Dear Ch...

A Journey int... ...er
A Collection of Angels & Miracles
A Celebration of Motherhood...

A Book for Bereaved Parents and for those who Love Them

Edition V

By Joanne Cacciatore- Garard

_____

_____

In Loving Memory Of:

_____

"*There are times when sorrow seems to be the only truth.*"
Oscar Wilde, De Profundis

DEAR CHEYENNE
A Journey into grief
A Collection of angels and miracles
A celebration of motherhood
By Joanne Cacciatore

Cover Illustration by Linda Schmidt
In memory of her precious sweet baby boy, Skyler Kirby Schmidt
October 25, 1999- January 4, 2000
Remembered in the hearts of his family
A special thank you to Shaun and Heather Farrier in loving memory of Aaron Lee
Farrier, Jami Rae Garrison in memory of Lois Ellen Miller, and Angela Iverson in memory
of Cody Elijah Iverson

Publisher: M.I.S.S.
Copyright 1996,1997,1999, 2002
All rights reserved internationally

For more information visit the website at
www.missfoundation.org

to reorder copies send check or money order to:
M.I.S.S. Foundation
PO Box 5333
Peoria, Arizona   85385
Helping Families Facing Death...

Include $11.95 per copy plus $3.00 shipping

ISBN 0-9717266-5-5
Manufactured in the United States of America
Cacciatore, Joanne
Title 1

From the Author

I would like to thank my surviving children: **Arman**, my first born, spirited child and first true love; **Cameron**, my quiet and strong son who brightens my day with his beautiful blue eyes; **Stevie Jo**, my daughter for her love, courage, and infinite wisdom of the ages; **Joshua Cheyne**, my subsequent child and the light of my life. You have all given me hope and happiness in my life once again. Thanks to my friend **Jami** and her mom, **Lois**, in heaven, and our **Board of Directors** for your love and support. Thank you **Rob** for your friendship, wisdom, and endless volunteer hours. And to **Rusty** who came into our lives and supported our cause, helping change the world we live in. Thank you to **Randy**, my special Angel and my ray of sunshine and encouragement. And my endless gratitude to **David**, for his never-ending support, patience, and for believing in me. To all my professors at **Arizona State University** for believing in me, putting up with my incessant questions, and guiding me, thank you.

I also want to thank the true initiates, our **MISS Foundation families**, who have experienced the death of their child. Thank you to the **Compassionate Friends**- you helped me find the strength to evolve through this journey. Only those who have walked this path can understand the depth of this pain. It is my hope that in reading this book, you will allow yourself to experience the myriad of emotions of grief: from the denial, anger, blame, guilt and sadness to the resolution, fortitude, faith, and acceptance. We do not ever "get over" the death of our child. It is a lifetime journey that we must yield to when our hearts speak.

And words cannot express my thanks to my dearest friend and mentor, **Dr. Elisabeth Kubler-Ross**, the woman who planted the seed of compassion in my heart and who inspires me each day to continue this work. I love you, Elisabeth. I promise I will fight the good fight for the rights of grieving children and their families. I will listen for your guidance from the other side...

"Those who can't hear the music, think the dancer mad."

For my mother, Jo, who joined her granddaughter on November 4, 2001,
And for our beautiful Cheyenne-
Her beauty has forever changed our world.
I will never forget you, baby. See you on the other side.

Dear Cheyenne,
A Journey into Grief
A Collection of Love, Faith & Miracles
A Celebration of Motherhood

Proceeds from the sale of this book benefit
The M.I.S.S. Foundation Family Outreach Programs
For its dedication to assisting families
after the death of a child
and in the training of medical professionals who care for them.

623.979.1000
joanne@missfoundation.org
Or visit our website at www.missfoundation.org

Cacciatore, Joanne
ISBN 0-09717266-5-5

CONTENTS

Manifesto of My Grieving Heart, Mother's Day, 2002

This is my path. It was not a path of my choice, but it is a path I must walk with careful consideration. It is a journey through grief that takes time. It is a process that will drain my resources and my energy. I may be impatient and unfocused. I may get angry easily. I won't smile as often as I used to. Smiling hurts now. It never used to. Most everything hurts now, even breathing. Please be gentle with me.

I will not ever "get over it" so please don't urge me down that path. Even if it seems like I am having a good day, maybe I am even able to smile for a moment, the pain is just beneath the surface of my skin. Every cell in my body aches. The guilt is debilitating. My chest has a nearly constant sinking pain and sometimes I feel as if I will explode from the grief. This is affecting me as a woman, a wife, a mother, a human being. It affects every aspect of my psyche: spiritually, physically, mentally, and emotionally. I barely recognize myself in the mirror anymore. In fact, I am certain that I died the day my child died.

Remember that grief is as personal to each individual as a fingerprint. Don't tell me how I should or shouldn't be doing it or when I should or shouldn't be feeling 'better by now.' Don't tell me what's right or wrong. I'm doing it my way, in my time. If I am to survive this, I must do what is best for me.

Survival is a part of seeing life's meaning differently. What I knew to be true or absolute has been challenged so my perspectives are changing. Things that once seemed important to me are barely thoughts any longer. I notice hungry children now. I notice the homeless and the destitute. A mother's harsh voice toward her young child and an elderly person struggling with the door capture my attention. Shoeless children call out to me and I seem to cry constantly at all the injustice in the world.

Don't tell me that "God has a plan" for me. That seems easy to say coming from a person who tucks their own child into a safe, warm bed at night: Whose idea of "goodbye" is dropping their child off at school for the day. Can you begin to imagine *your* own child, flesh of your flesh, lying lifeless in a casket, when "goodbye" means you'll never see them on this earth again? This is not a transitory experience. I won't wake up one day with everything 'okay' and life back to normal. I have a new sense of normal now. Life has let me down in a way I never imagined it would. I believe that this cruel joke of Mother Nature will affect me for the rest of my life.

Oh, perhaps as time passes, I will discover new meanings and insights about what my child's death means to me. Perhaps, one day, when I am very, very old, I will say that time has truly helped to heal my broken heart. But always remember that not a day passes without thoughts of my deceased child, no matter how many years have passed. Love never dies.

And this year, on Mother's Day, don't forget that I have another one, another child, albeit invisible to your eye. Don't forget to say, "How are you *really* feeling this Mother's Day?" Don't forget that even if I have living children, my heart still aches for the one that is absent. *For I am never quite complete without my child.*

Prologue

I am not certain if I believe in destiny. Most days, I vacillate in wonder...

What I do know is that there is a shroud of silence surrounding death in our society. I have never really understood why. There are two common human experiences that transcend culture, region, religion, ethnicity, and socio-economic status. Two absolutes that every person on earth will face: birth and death. Birth is celebrated and embraced in our society. Many people plan well in advance for the birth of their child. Death is another story. It seems our culture supports the ideal that if we ignore death, it will not affect us. If we find quaint euphemisms or platitudes to describe death or to comfort those who mourn, then no one will have to feel the grief.

I hate platitudes. You know, those ignorant things people will say to make you feel better after your loved one dies. "God has a plan for you," or "You're young, you can try again." More recently, after learning of the work I have committed to since Cheyenne's death, people say things like, "You see, everything happens for a reason..."

Perhaps. But I don't have to like it.

I wonder, each day of this journey that I travel, if this was really *supposed* to happen to me. The many things that have changed because of Chey's life and death have truly been astonishing. This little infant who no one else really knew has changed so many lives. The reality of the whole event and the resultant grief is still overwhelming nearly eight years later.

Yet, I realized that whether it was destiny or not, whether this experience was part of some master plan to impel me, in some small way, to educate our culture about death or not, it doesn't really matter. I don't like the reality that I faced in 1994 and that I face each day without Cheyenne in my life. Parents should never bury their own child...it seems a cruel joke of Mother Nature.

But I have a choice between the roads that I take: the road to apathy or the road to fortitude. I believe apathy leads to repressed emotions and unhealthy grieving. I believe fortitude brings miracles and social change. Whether or not this was destiny is immaterial at this point. I have made my choice of roads and that choice has been the best for me. It has shown me that one person truly can change the world...even if that person has died.

Passages...

A pink stripe-positive, innocent unknowing,
Destiny prevails
Screaming, "This shall be!"
Ten lunar months
With or without her participation

She engages in the battle of denim
The expanding belly- The Victor!
Tearful quest
For acceptance of herself
And elastic waistbands, instead

Danger: Nicotine. She smells it.
Looking for the source, nearby
Quickly changing seats
She drowns in primitive awareness
The role of sentinel

Tup-tup, tup-tup, tup-tup
Their eyes dance to the beat
Of their unborn sister's heart
Smiles
Anticipation
Hope
Patience
Lessons esoteric
And then off to the sandbox

What is happening?
Could it be? A gesture of life
Maybe just her stomach? Must be indigestion-
No! Again...the flutter of her baby.
No words. Just silence and a moment. A sacred moment.
Tear-beads accessorize the day.

Dancing bears and mint green lambs
Adorn the walls
The bassinet awaits to become the warm, safe place
Second only to the nest of her arms
Three weeks remain
She travels down roads of visual imagery
The sterile room
Pain, the joy...the incredible moment of birth
Her heart beats, races without ease
Deleting calendar days in her mind
But serenity steps in the door, and brings a morsel of patience along

3

Barely re-transitioned
To the repose of slumber
Her only escape from the suffering
2:00 a.m., six pillows and bathroom run three
Tiredness creeps in
Stolen reserves
Her ankle bones hiding beneath the swollen tissue
Sacrifice of self. Trapped in this foreign body. Vulnerable. Frightened.
Naked and aching
The journey has taken its toll

Two more days
An eternity, at least
She gently strokes her abdomen unaware
As their hands meet with holy intimacy-
She knows her mother. Better than anyone. They are one.
Love, only love, wakes her slumber

Morning saunter is slow
But this day will be different
She falls to her knees as if to pray
A pain, indescribable
Her body convulses
"Oh my, God!"
Too fast...it is all too fast.
Rushing, rushing...get the doctor
"She is term, contractions every minute...she'll be going soon!"
Excited, yes, but scared too! It is happening so fast.
Culmination of timeless time will soon end. Her laborious months
Finally yielding the reward

"It was all worth it," she thinks silently

She smiles through the pain, with renewed assurance that it will all be over soon
A hodgepodge of clinicians, in and out
Unrecognizable faces sharing in the moment
Schooled by choice to be surrounded with new life
With brazen confidence the man who will guide
the passage from the womb's safety meets her glance
Strapping charcoal bands, cold, tight
Around the infants swollen domicile

Sudden change. Faces transform. Silence-
Their smiles break like glass
Searing through the faces of the white costumed staff
Glances unfamiliar to her
Once again, her body not her own

"What is happening?"

4

Silence-

They team up. Together. Screaming repetitions of nothingness
"What is happening!?"

Their secret code fractures her spirit.
Fear begins to ravage every cell in her body

His heart is callused like a laborer's hands
The synopsis, detached
"Your baby is dead."
                              "Your baby is dead."
                              "Your baby is dead."
                              "Your baby is dead."
"Your baby is dead." (*Please, please turn the volume down.*)

Contractions every thirty seconds
No time to think. No La Maze. Too much pain.
Unimaginable pain
Physical. Spiritual. Mental. Emotional.
"What? No. No. No. No. NO!"
She tries to get up from the bed

They hold her down, like a prisoner
What crime has she committed?

"No. I cannot do this. I want her to stay within me. Safe and warm...
No. I do not want to have my baby now! Let me go home. Lies, all lies!"

She fights in hateful protest-
But the contractions bound her, and kick her,
And punish her.

Corrosive sweat
Rains like fire from her temples

"Push, push, push."
She can feel her child being born.

Head, elbows, chest. Finally her feet emerge
From her Judas body
Someone puts the camera on slow motion.
Frame by frame, outside herself she watches

Eyes clenched tight

Awaiting, baited breath.

"Cry, baby. Cry for mommy," she pleads helplessly

Negotiations. What can I give? What sacrifice? My life? Money? Time?
She is gone.

"What is happening? I do not understand. PLEASE take me! Take me!" she implores
No one throws her the lifejacket. She drowns in agony, and
Dresses her lifeless baby in bear pajamas that match her room
The pajamas say, "I love mommy" all over
But mommy has failed. Mommy couldn't save you.

Pink, white, and blue are the choices
Not for lacy dresses but for caskets- they ask her to choose. "Choose? A casket?"
Looking around, planning her escape
For there are too many tiny caskets in the room closing in
She cannot see, as the tears asphyxiate her
Falling to the cold tile
"This cannot be, this cannot be."

The second hand is in a hurry today.
She begs it to stop, but the time has come.
Reluctantly she places her into the pastel casket
Carefully, as she bends over to kiss this child of Heaven

Milk burns at her breast in disapproval
Her body doesn't understand
Her body must feed her, hold her, nurture her
A visceral need unfulfilled

Beautiful- eight pounds, dark curly hair, porcelain baby
She closes the casket cover
And falls down in fetal position
One being. She remembers when they were one-
A loss so physical, so permanent

Now death has transplanted her organs with despair
Today, she will bury her precious child.
Cathedral flowers tied with ribbons of sorrow
Black limousines stand at attention
Her anesthetized consciousness fades
In and out, as the sun dances
Between summer clouds

And from the earth that swallows her child
She begs acquittal

Stepping in to assume the role her body once played so well
Her mind becomes the stranger now
Evolution, bursting, dragging her through the muddy waters of grief
Swallowing the poison,
Blinding her, confusing her

Senseless propaganda in her ears
Stinging reminders around every corner
Disinterring the immortal hours...
Her body bleeds defiantly, still,
And her spirit lay mortally wounded
Amongst the shadows
Curled up
On the dark closet floor
Where her elastic-waisted garments hanged,
Anointed with French vanilla

And where no one witnessed
As she invited Death to come.
But He declined her offer
Another time, perhaps?
He leaves her in the carnage.

Like Gretel, looking for crumbs of hope
To guide her through the forest,
Through the passages of the deepest torment she will ever know
Not one in the millions
Of peoples, languages or philosophies
Can begin to speak the truth of
The torment of a mother
Whose child has been ripped, without mercy
From her burning arms

2,190 days
Six phantom years but love does not decompose as flesh
Memories try to sneak away when she is not looking,
The alarm sounds and quickly she brings them home
Edges of the photographs are time-faded and worn from too much handling

So she juxtaposes scenes from two worlds
And escapes to the voices of a thousand ghosts

Yet, in the underground passages of her mind
Through the only pardon from darkness
Shines the light of hope
And the gifts of angels, immortal

Now she walks the forests thick with grief
Leaving crumbs for the others
To discover the passage to peace and courage
To discover and to help change the world.
Destiny prevails
And whispers, "This shall be!"

July 27, 2000

7

The Journey Begins . . .

The sky blue nursery was already prepared for you. It seemed like the longest of all my pregnancies. I had hoped for another little girl. But according to the ultrasound, you were a boy. It didn't matter. I loved you anyway, my fourth child. Everyone always joked about me being the proverbial overprotective, health nut of the family, cautious about even chewing gum with aspartame. Regardless, I continued my healthy vegetarian diet throughout my pregnancy with you, just as I had done with the other three.

But when I arrived at the hospital in transitional labor on July 27, 1994, something went terribly wrong. I was already eight centimeters dilated and without any pain medication I am trying to get through my fourth natural childbirth. It seemed that my labor with you was more painful than with the others. I quickly learned why. About ten minutes after we arrived at the hospital, the doctors told me they thought you had died. I lay there in disbelief. I kept asking if I could just go home. I knew this could not be true. I knew you were alive and that the doctors were wrong. It seemed like hours in that room. Everyone was so quiet. Still disbelieving their continued diagnosis, I convinced myself that you would prove them wrong. My son would come out screaming and we would all shout for joy!

They were asking me silly questions, hundreds of them. They asked if I wanted to hold you. They asked if I wanted pictures of you. But I am trying to concentrate on giving birth with the contractions now one minute apart. Anyway, babies don't die during labor anymore. It just doesn't happen. Within twenty minutes after I arrived at the hospital, I gave birth. My eyes closed tight, they handed you to your father. He loosened the blanket in the silence of that sterile hospital room. But you did not cry or even attempt to breathe. They offered no explanation, nor any reason. The doctor said there was none. There was only the deafening stillness in that room. Not knowing what to expect, I was afraid to look at you. This was my first experience with death. My body trembled with fear and adrenaline.

But then with my eyes still held tightly shut, your father gasped as he unraveled the blanket. He told me that I had a little girl. I sat up in disbelief and grabbed you, my daughter, my little girl. You are what I had hoped for all along. I looked at your perfect, lifeless body. You were so beautiful. Your skin was flawless and you had curly, ebony hair. You were my largest newborn, weighing 8 lbs. and certainly the healthiest appearing of all my children. You had a double chin and rolls of fat around your soft wrists. That made it so difficult to understand what happened. You looked like you were asleep. I remember being tempted to breathe life into you but fear of intervention from the medical staff prevented me from trying. With a mother's love, I instinctively knew I had to make my first and last memories with you now.

I looked over at your father. He had been crying for awhile now. But I had not yet begun to cry. I just held you in my aching arms and kissed you gently. I felt overcome with love and helplessness, happiness and sorrow. The intensity of my emotions surprised me.

The silence was horrifying. The nurse and doctor quickly left the room. I held you and cried a little, but I still had not accepted this as reality. For two broken hours, I dressed you, took pictures, and kissed you hundreds of times. I unraveled you from your blanket every fifteen minutes to examine and reexamine every inch of your body. I wriggled your toes, caressed your arms, and stroked your soft warm cheeks. As your tiny body began to blister, they urged me to let them take you to be prepared for the mortuary. Reluctantly, I handed you to the nurse and said goodbye.

Knowing I could not stay in the hospital a moment longer, I left for home. For forty weeks I planned my life around you. I loved you and nurtured you inside me. My every waking thought was consumed with waiting for your arrival. For forty long weeks, I changed the way I ate, the way I dressed, the movies I watched, and my every thought and word. All of this for nothing. As I headed toward the exit, I walked past the nursery with my empty arms and broken heart. I was leaving the hospital without you. That is when I began the very difficult and boundless journey into grief. I had no idea the pain I was about to experience. I chose the name, Cheyenne; it means 'white mourning dove.'

Little child of mine
On this day, you died
And you have taken with you more than your own life
You have taken my life too.
I died with you today.
You have changed my life forever.

Thirty Three Hours

It is 3:04 a.m.
Only 33 hours since your birth...
    And your death.
But it seems an eternity.

Still I hope to awaken from this nightmare
To find myself pregnant
And complaining about your knee in my rib, again.

I have always known
That losing a child
Is the most difficult experience for a parent to endure.
Yet I never expected the pain would be as deep as it is.

So I live and relive the hours before your birth and death
Wondering,
    Was it something I ate?
      Or lifted or said?
Desperately clinging to theories on
Why you couldn't hold onto life.

I only know that from the moment of your miraculous existence
Inside of me,
I loved you intensely.

Just as the other three whom I so deeply love
I also loved and needed you.

So each day we dreamed and planned for your future.
    Your kindergarten class
    Graduation
    College
    Your wedding day.
Even your own children. But we never planned for your death.
Now, I ache for you
Beautiful Cheyenne.
My arms long desperately to hold you and to love you.

I long to kiss your soft skin and stroke your cheek as I nurse you at my breast.
I long to rock you to sleep and sing you the raindrops on roses song
(It is your big sister's favorite)

I long to watch you sleeping peacefully

To see you growing everyday,
    Playing with your sister and brothers,
Filling our days with your laughter and our nights with your love.

I long to take you on walks to the park.
I long to see the glimmering sun in your beautiful eyes.

I long to awaken you every morning
            With a smile and a kiss (or two)

But your death has left me with an empty womb and a broken heart.
Wondering if the sun will ever shine again
        Or if the sparrow's song will ever sound as sweet.

Wondering if each and every smile will always be this painful
And each tear as heart wrenching.

And though others may,
            I will not forget you, little girl.
Nor do I wish to try.

I will love you and keep you
        Close to my heart
                Until my last
                        Dying breath...

Forever Yours,

Mommy

July 29, 1994

I still have not slept a minute, Cheyenne. I feel numb. I feel like a zombie. I cannot remember anything. I keep losing my keys and forgetting to brush my teeth. I still feel so confused. There are so many questions and yet there are no answers. I don't even know why you died.

I don't understand. It just doesn't make sense. I don't drink or smoke. I take my vitamins and herbs. I eat healthy food and exercise in moderation. I am a good mother and I love my children deeply. I take care of them. I love being a mother. Why me? Why my baby? We waited so long for you. We made a place for you in our home and in our hearts.

I am sure I will wake up soon. Yes, this is all just a very bad nightmare. I want to wake up. Can someone please help me?

I must be patient with myself
Kind to myself
Loving to myself
I must allow myself time
To feel and experience
To accept this
New road I am on

Yes, I must be patient with myself
For the road I now travel
Is a long and destructive one

I must take my time along the way
Please do not rush my journey

July 31, 1994

It has been four days since your death. Sleep is sporadic, at the most one or two hours a night. I do not like to sleep. When I wake up groggy, I convince myself that it was just a dream and then feel relieved. But then I look down at my empty womb and I am jolted back into this hell I am living.

We went to the mortuary today. I got to hold you for hours on the couch alone. I wish that there were a rocking chair in that room. I would love to rock you. I am going to buy a nightgown for you to be buried in. Aunt Mandy had a special blanket knit for you even before you were born. We will wrap you in it. Your Grandma Priscilla came in from New Mexico and we realized how much you look like her. We sat around the mortuary most of the day, trying our best to get through until tomorrow. Grandma and Grandpa Cacciatore, Auntie Eda and a few friends came by for the visitation. I want it to be special for our family. I hope they will take this time to get to know you, too. I do not ever want them to forget you.

Your father and I got into an argument on the way home. I don't remember why, but it doesn't seem to matter now. Nothing matters. I cannot watch television. I cannot stand to hear music. I do not want to be around anyone at all. No one can understand how I feel inside. There are no words and no amount of tears that can express the depth of the agony. I cannot eat.

My breasts ache. They are full with your milk. My head hurts from thinking too much. My eyes burn from the tears. My arms ache to hold you.

I feel alone - all alone on an island. Can't anyone hear me? Can't anyone feel the depth of my pain?

Cry out, my soul
You have good reason
Do not apologize for your sorrow or your tears
To yourself or to others
Cry out from depths beyond comprehension
Maybe then - they will feel your abysmal pain
And maybe then - someone, somewhere will hear you.

August 1, 1994

We went back to the mortuary today. This is the day we will bury you.

We brought the video camera and took many of pictures of you. I think everyone was mortified that we brought the video camera. It doesn't matter though. This is my only chance to make memories with you. It is my last chance to say goodbye. If I do not make this time with you, I will never be able to get it back. And while I know your spirit is not here, I already miss your little body being close to me. I am still a mother. I am still *your* mother.

I wonder if I should have brought the children here with me. I am scared for them and feel I have to protect them. Deep inside I don't feel this is right. They should be here with me saying goodbye to you too. I am sure I am going to regret not having them here. Cheyenne, why did this happen to us? It is so unfair. Someone told me that 'I was young, and could have more children.' I don't want any other child- I want you!

We placed pictures of your family, your rattles and toys, and your blanket in the casket to be buried with you. I bought a special nightgown which I dressed you in. I wanted you to look warm and comfortable. I became very upset because the pillow was too large for your little head. I started to sob as I yanked the stuffing out of the pillow uncontrollably. The funeral director and your Father just stood back and allowed me to be your mother, as I frantically tried to make your bed right for you.

When I finally calmed down, I held you on the couch, peacefully, for most of the morning. Then they came in and told me it was time. Time to take you to the cemetery. Time to say our final good byes.

I lay you in your little bed, gently, and I cried as I closed the casket.

This cannot be the last time
For us to share together
Our love is too deep, Too real
This cannot be good bye

A hot summer day
August of '94

Hotter than I'd ever felt before

As sweat
And tears pour from my cheeks
I bury my little girl.

In a tiny, pink satin casket
Surrounded with sweetheart roses
Encircled with pictures of her mourning family.

I watch as shovel by shovel
The men in gray suits
Covered her tender body with dirt.
My heart screaming with pain.

Good-bye.
We say good-bye.

August 14, 1994

Dear Cheyenne,

Last night was horrible. The monsoons came. I heard the lightning and ran to the window. I sat on the couch and heard the rain suddenly pour down. Panicked, I realized that your fragile little body would become drenched. I grabbed a raincoat and headed for the garage. I don't know what came over me at that very moment but I was determined to go to the cemetery, get you, and protect you from the rain. I looked for the shovel and just as I found it with my keys in hand, tears pouring from my eyes, your father pulled me back into the house. I fought him, yelled at him to let me go. I tried to explain that I *had* to go and get you. It was my *job*. To protect you from harm. Oh Cheyenne, none of this makes any sense. How could this happen?

This great undertaking
Grief.
I don't believe I have the power
To face it alone
To conquer the helplessness, the desperation, the agony
For the first time in my life
I realized
That I need others

September 2, 1994

I am completely exhausted with this grief. I am sure I have cried an ocean of tears. I receive flowers and cards everyday, even from strangers. I think it is the saddest when a child dies. It is not supposed to happen this way, Cheyenne. A parent should always die before their child. It is out of the natural order of life.

Your death certificate and autopsy report came in the mail today. I called vital records to get your birth certificate - I really have no use or desire for your death certificate. To my great surprise, they told me that because you died just prior to your birth, I would not receive a birth certificate. When I argued their reasoning, she told me that I 'didn't have a baby.' She said I had a 'fetus' and that 'the fetus died.' It was like someone stuck a knife in my back. I hung up the phone and cried for two hours.

I feel like my body failed. I feel like my body killed you. The guilt is incalculable. You lived and died inside of me. I am so sorry. Everyday I run through the list of "would've, should've and could've," thinking I should have known or been able to do something to prevent this.

The results back from the pathologist offered no explanation. He diagnosed your cause of death as 'undetermined.' Everything was perfect or so he says. So here I am again, left searching for an answer. But even an answer won't bring you back. I pace the floors at night, like a wild animal searching for its infant who was ripped from the safety its mother- my body craving yours. It is just so lonely inside this pain. It is the most seclusion I have ever known.

It seems that this is larger than I am
More than I can handle
Yet I know that I am being carried
For I am not strong enough
To carry myself

I do not have the answers now
But one day I will know
And understand
And maybe one day
I will help to carry another

Cheyenne's Lullaby

Sleep, Our Little Angel
Let Golden Slumbers Fill Your Eyes

Sleep Our Little Angel
As We Try To Say Good-bye

Sleep Our Little Angel
As These Memories Rare and Few

Are a Bittersweet Remembrance
Of a Love So Painfully True

Sleep Our Precious Daughter
For Your Beauty Was Too Deep

In Our Hearts You Live, Forever
Sleep Our Little Angel,
Sleep...

September 5, 1994

This weekend Auntie Eda bought me a weekend at the Boulders Resort in Carefree, Arizona. My family believes that if I stay busy, I won't think about you. But they are wrong. I love to think about you. I need to remember you. It is so hard to understand that when you are outside of the grief. They want to take the pain away because they love me. What they do not realize is that I need this pain. It is all I have. They think if they don't talk about you, I will not be sad. What they do not realize is that when they avoid speaking about you, it magnifies the anguish, and my disconnectedness.

By Sunday afternoon, I could not stand the isolation of being out of town any longer. We headed back towards Phoenix. Knowing the only thing that helps ease the grief is a visit to the cemetery, we stopped at Paradise Memorial Gardens to bring you pink roses.

There are many children buried here. I cry not only for my pain, but also for the pain that I know so many other parents must endure. One particular boy, 'Timothy James' (nicknamed Peter Pan on his headstone), captured my attention. On every visit to the cemetery, I have always felt drawn towards his area. I spend a lot of time tending his grave. I left a dozen pink roses and a small stuffed bear for you, and one for Timmy also.

I then commented that someday I would like to meet Timmy's mom.

Miracles happen to each of us everyday
But we must open our mind and spirit
In order to receive them...

September 6, 1994

Tonight was the first day of the grief support group meeting, Compassionate Friends. We arranged to go to the meeting at 7:00 p.m. It was held only one mile from our home. We walked into the room and began to meet a group of about twenty other grieving parents. Most of the parents shared pictures of their children. I didn't bring a picture of you because I didn't know what to expect. There was so much pain in the room, I wasn't sure if I would be able to stay.

As I was looking at all the pictures, one particular child's photo brought tears to my eyes. He was a sweet, blonde-hair boy. I held onto his picture for a long time, staring bewilderingly at it; hypnotized by his photograph. As each parent told their story, I cried with them. I began to recognize that the people in this room felt my pain. It brought a sense of comfort to me realizing that I wasn't alone on this journey; that others too, deeply mourned the death of their child. When the parents of the older children spoke, I felt envy because they had pictures of their children alive. They had twenty, thirty, or forty years with their child to get to know them. They were able to share the joys of being their parent. They had an opportunity to make memories with that child. They were able to discover their child's personality. They knew their child's favorite food and their favorite color. Some even had grandchildren. Yet we all had so much in common.

I realized that feeling cheated out of any time with my daughter intensified this grief. I never had the chance to look into her eyes or tell her how much I loved her. I never got to walk her to her first day of kindergarten, or down the aisle for her wedding day. How can a person die before they are even born? It makes no sense at all. How unfair can life be? But while I found myself envying those who had more time with their children, I realized that a child should never die at any age. One mother began her story, sharing about her son. He died at age two and she had never been given a satisfactory answer for the cause of his death. She then pointed out to me that her son was the boy in the picture which had so mesmerized me. As she continued to talk about him, I realized that this was Timmy's mom, the little boy who is buried at Cheyenne's cemetery. Thinking my imagination had gone wild, I asked her where he was buried. I was right! She was the one I that I wanted to meet. I never imagined I would meet her today. I told her that I was the one who had been leaving things at his grave. We hugged each other and cried. She told me that I helped her immensely. She felt such joy that someone else cared enough to leave things at his grave and care for his sacred burial place. Every person in the room had goose bumps.

Our paths have crossed for a reason
Let us grieve together, remember together, share together, heal together...
For no one else can understand the depth of this heartache
No one else is willing to hear the painful truth
About the love and about the pain
Of our precious child

October 27, 1994

It has been three months since your death. I think the shock is finally wearing off. It is starting to sink in that I will never see you again. We won't be together in this lifetime. I cannot negotiate the terms of this contract.

People have stopped sending cards and flowers. They have stopped offering their support and their condolences. They say it's time for me to move on. They say I must go forward in my life. It is time to "put it all behind me." They say it is "better this way" and that "everything happens for a reason." They tell me, "God has a plan for you." They say it is better that you died at birth, rather than at six months. They tell me to be grateful for the three children I have.

I have always been thankful my other children. I adore all four of my children! What does being grateful for my three surviving children have to do with my sadness over losing you? Does it mean that I should not feel horrible if I lose one of my children? An enormous part of our family is missing. These words cut like a knife and I don't understand why people say these horrible things. Maybe it is because they are trying to make themselves feel comfortable with the death of a baby. I don't know. They do not understand. I am so very frustrated. If God's plan included the death of their child, I wonder how willing they would be to accept and "get over it."

Love me and care for me
Be my friend
Be available to listen
Do not respond, only listen
For words do not heal
Hug me and tell me
That this horrible injustice
Should never happen
And let me share my pain
Without reproach or condition
Do not run from me
Or leave the room when I say her name
Hold my hand and share her memory
Love does not end with death...

November 16, 1994

Today is my birthday. I do not want to celebrate anything, Cheyenne. I feel like a part of me is missing. One minute I can be laughing and playing with your sister and your brothers, and the next minute something hits me and I fall apart. I grieve so deeply that it is physically painful. My throat and my chest ache - well, it is unbearable.

Some people don't seem to help much either. I am not speaking to Sandy, even though we have been good friends for five years. She called yesterday and asked me what was wrong. I told her I was crying because it is my birthday tomorrow and my daughter is not here to celebrate with me. She said, *"Joanne, you need to accept this as God's will in your life and move on."* What ignorance! I couldn't believe she said that. She doesn't even have children. She doesn't know about the love of a mother or the miracle of nurturing a child within your womb. She can't begin to comprehend the bittersweet pain of childbirth. She doesn't know that the only thing that makes forty weeks of pregnancy worth all the pain and effort is the reward at the end of the pregnancy. How dare she say that to me? I hung up on her. I am in enough pain: I don't need shallow consoling now.

I am so angry about the senseless comments and platitudes. I know people have good intentions, but they wound deeply with their tenebrous attempts at justifying your death. I have made a decision that from now on when someone makes an unreasonable comment in an attempt to comfort me I am going to tell that person why it hurts.

Today I did just that. Someone told me that what happened was "meant to be" because something was probably wrong with you. I told him that if you were less than perfect, I would have loved you even more. He just stood there unable to speak a word. He quickly realized how very foolish his words were and that they did much more harm than good. Speaking out is the only way I can handle it anymore. While I probably caused him some emotional discomfort, I am sure he will think before he speaks. People should think what they say, not say what they think.

Love is unconditional
Love knows no boundaries
Especially the bond of love between a parent
and a child....

It transcends human comprehension
It transcends reason, rationale
Even death
It is eternal...

My Child Has Died

My Child has died.
Do not tell me it may be for the best
Or that all things happen for a reason
My dreams are buried with her.
This unthinkable, unspeakable tragedy
Has become my reality.

I will never be who I once was.

My child has died.
Do not attempt to comfort with mere mortal words
Or spiritual delights
Nothing else matters now
And this pain within my heart
Cannot heal with a band-aid or a kiss.

So, please, do not try to take away the grief
It is all that remains
It is the only emotion I can feel
And do not inquire of my condition
I cannot answer with shallow words

My child has died.
But as the world continues on in absolute oblivion,
Please, pause a moment...
Do not urge me to abandon her memory.
Offer your kindness.
Speak to my soul with gentle words.
Offer your condolences with compassion filled eyes
For her brief life was worthy of my pain and your remembrance.

My child has died.
But not in senseless vanity
Allow her to bring you closer to those you love
Discover through her existence how truly fragile life is.
Share with me her memory.
Her name is Cheyenne.

November 22, 1994

Your Auntie Eda decided I needed to speak to a family counselor, so reluctantly, I went. I spent about two hours there. It seemed he didn't have a clue how I was feeling or why my feelings were so profound. I brought some of my poetry, your pictures and your baby book. He was very surprised that I had gone through the effort to create a baby book and picture album and he seemed confused by my desire to hold on to you. He wanted to talk about other things and seemed to avoid really talking about your death but I needed to talk about it. I wanted to understand why it hurt so much and why no one else could validate the pain.

I was very frustrated because he kept generalizing the grief I feel. It is not the same as other grief- I feel disenfranchised. Out of absolute frustration, I asked him about his family life. I thought surely he wasn't a parent and that was the reason he could not relate to my sadness as parent. To my surprise, he said he had three children and that his wife was pregnant with their fourth child. I left feeling violated and angry that he could not justify the depth of my grief. I also told him that I hoped he would never have to experience in his own life.

I will never go back there again. The only ones who seem to understand are the people in our TCF group. Sharing with other grieving parents is far more therapeutic to me than a counselor who cannot validate or understand the grief of a mother who is mourning.

I cannot wait until our next support group meeting. It seems that month-to-month, it is the only thing that keeps me going. Being able to communicate with others who feel my pain and truly understand that saying goodbye to your child is not the same as saying goodbye to anyone else in your life.

There are no words in the English language
Which can express the depth of this pain, guilt, anger, & sorrow
How can I possibly cope?
Perhaps, by realizing that your life is worthy
Of every emotion that I feel
Every sleepless night that I face
And each teardrop that falls.

December 12, 1994

It seems you are on my mind every minute of every hour of every day. People think that because I do not wear dark sunglasses or black clothes I am over you and finished with my grief work. But this feeling of helplessness is all consuming, and besides...

I will never, ever get over you. I don't want to get over you. You are a part of me and who I am. If I tried to forget you or go on as if nothing had ever happened, certainly I would feel as if I had not only betrayed you but also betrayed myself. They say that when you lose a parent, you lose your past; when you lose a spouse, you lose your present; and when you lose a child, you lose your future. I disagree. The day you died, I lost my past, my present, and my future. My life will never be the same.

I think I have come to a point in my grief, however, where I am able to reflect back and smile, remembering how beautiful you were. It is such a strange feeling to be a proud mother of such a beautiful daughter and at the same exact moment feel horrified that I will live the rest of my life without being able to share it with you.

For the rest of my life, until the day I die, I will think of you. I will remember. Remembering you is all I have left to do.

The loss of a child
Is bitter
But the memory of that child
Is sweet
Hold on to the memory
Experience the sweetness
For that child
Is forever your child

Seasons

I will think of you in summer
As the sanctuary of night becomes obscure
The blistering heat of the sun
Reminds me of the pain of the summer of '94.

I will think of you in autumn
As the trees become a potpourri of colors
The leaves begin to fall
As freely as the tears.

I will think of you in winter
When the earth's brilliant canvas
Dims in the cold, bitter breeze
In spite of my protest, the cycle continues
For Mother Earth does not stop to hear my cries

But then, the renewing blossoms
Call to the coming season
Of the celestial night
And I will kneel at your grave
        Look unto the stars
                And whisper your name

And the resonance of your memory fills
My vacant heart
For that very moment, with undying devotion,
I will celebrate your existence
I will think of you
I will remember you
In hopeful shroud of spring.

December 22, 1994

I started my new job last week. It is very demanding and takes a lot of concentration. I have learned a good lesson about grieving. The lesson is that I must do it! It seems that when I prolong the grief or keep my days so full that I do not have any quiet time to do my grief work. It reminds me of a bank loan. The longer I take to repay the loan, the higher the interest rate plus penalties.

I have been holding back the past few days and the stress it is creating has become apparent in my behavior at home. I have been short tempered and feel like exploding at times. Your father has not been crying much lately, and I am beginning to feel more and more isolated. My anger toward him is difficult to control. Sometimes my emotions are frightening.

I think I will go to the cemetery tomorrow, Cheyenne. It is a wonderful and serene place for me to cry and to allow myself to grieve. I think everyone needs to have that safe place to go and meditate. It is amazing what a good hard cry does for me. I feel like someone has lifted a huge weight off my shoulders when I allow myself that time.

A quiet place to go
Where God can whisper words
Of comfort and reassurance
Without distractions
Without judgments
A safe haven for tears
A place to fall apart
And to regain composure
We all need that place
That quiet place to go...

Dear Cheyenne,

I am thinking of you again, little one
And the stinging in my heart for you continues.
But for that I am thankful.

They said, "Time will heal,"
But time has not been good to me
It has only made me love and miss you more.

Yet, recently I have realized that without your existence
I would not be who I have become today.

This supernatural strength which I have discovered
To endure this overwhelming pain and confusion
Is one of the many gifts you have given me.
For that I thank you.

You have transformed my life
Into a sea of vast and embellishing emotions
For that I thank you.

Because of you, I am able to love even deeper
Every moment of joy is a treasured celebration.

Now, and because of you,
I savor every moment in life, good and bad.

My compassion for others has become my allegiance
As I share in their pain and their tears.
When I grieve, the sorrow emanates from depths I have never known.
For that I thank you.

You have put life's wonders into perspective
Demanding that I see the colors of life
And taste the bitter with the sweet.
For that I thank you.

You do not allow me to forget
But have taught me to accept
        to remember
        and to remain faithful.

For that I thank you.

You have taught me the lessons of loving
and the pain of saying good-bye.

You are my greatest teacher of life and death
Experiencing both together
For that I thank you.

Each and every day,
I continue to discover you,
to know you,
to love you,
to understand you

And why you came into my life.

I love you, Cheyenne.

I will always be your Mommy and I will always love you.
For that, I thank you.

But you have given me more
In your brief existence
Than I could have given you
In a lifetime of being your Mommy.

For that, I thank you, Baby Girl.

Faithfully Yours,
Mommy

December 24, 1994

It is Christmas Eve. The children are going to Aunt Mandy's house for dinner and I planned a trip to Phoenix Children's Hospital. I had to do something more altruistic with the money that I would have used to buy your Christmas presents, so I bought some gifts to give to children. I chose eight girl presents and six boy presents. But then something amazing happened! As I headed downtown to my destination, I took a detour to John C. Lincoln Hospital. I don't know why I went there, but I did. I walked into the lobby and asked if there were any children at the hospital. She checked the patient list and, believe it or not, there were no children in the hospital. We were both pleased to discover that no children would have to spend Christmas Eve there.

I told her of my mission to distribute toys to children in need and she wished me well. As I headed toward the exit, I heard her yelling, "Miss, Miss!" I turned to see what she wanted. She told me of a Head Start program down the street that provided child-care to lower income families. Many of the parents would be working on Christmas Eve so she suggested I try there.

Taking her advice, I went to the Lincoln Learning Center. With my big bag of gifts, I entered the facility. The center director was very happy about my mission, explaining that many of these children may not receive gifts this year. I went into the room to hand out the toys. Incredibly, in the center that day, there were eight little girls and six little boys. The exact amount of toys that I had brought!

What a wonderful day! I am trying to take some of the anguish and transform it into some sense of joy for other children. Today, as I got into my car, crying with joy and sadness, I realized that I had done just that!

But my heart still aches for you. I love you, Cheyenne. I love you.

Never take life for granted
It is too brief
It is too precious
It is too fragile...

15 minutes more
And you would have been an infant
Not just a fetus
Worthy of the certificate-
Confirmation of your birth

15 minutes more
And you would have been a child
In their eyes
A sad statistic of mortality
Not merely an asterisk that no one sees

15 minutes more
For the birth certificate
(They can keep the death certificate)

They think that fifteen minutes
Is the difference between a fetus and a child.

They are dead wrong

You are my child
Born of my body and spirit
And I love you just as much as I would have
If you would have taken that breath of life
15 minutes more

Their trite justifications
'At least we didn't have time together'
And I should be glad I never brought you home.
And I think, silently- as the knife bends in my back,
"I would have given my life to bring you home and have some time with you."

Time to comfort you when you cried
Time to rock you to sleep when you were tired
Time to feed your hunger and quench your thirst
Time to ease your pain or fears
Time to know my little girl.
Time for my little girl to know me.
Time to be your mommy.
For 15 minutes more...

January 20, 1995

It seems like everyone has forgotten you and left me all alone in this agony. This is a nightmare.

> Part of me
> Is gone, dead
> How can I pretend that you never were?
> That I am okay
> That I am complete without you
> How can I cope when everyone has forsaken me
> And abandoned you?

January 21, 1995

I am having a horrible time. Today, I am falling apart. Like a puzzle with half the pieces missing, I cannot get it together, focus, or even think. I am haunted by thoughts of you. I wonder if you were frightened or if you felt any pain. Were you afraid? Did you die a peaceful death? I feel so helpless and out of control. I couldn't do anything to comfort you or to save you. I am so sorry, little girl. I would have given my life for yours that day. You died all alone inside of your mommy. The pain is so relentless. I want to feel your little arms around my neck.

I wanted to go out to the cemetery and my family asked me how long I am going to continue visiting the cemetery weekly. They said they didn't think it was 'good for me' anymore. I became very angry with them. We had a very long and emotional argument.

Recognizing how foolish it was to try and rush my healing, we cried together and they apologized. I think everyone wishes that we could forget about the experience. But I will never forget it. That would be forgetting you. All I can do is struggle through this grief work. It is mentally exhausting and physically tiring, but I know I must do it.

I try so hard to stay in control but that only seems to make it worse. I know I must surrender my heart and my mind to the grief. Fighting it only makes it harder. Last night, I spent my 12th night in a row crying in the corner, at 3 a.m., of the closet floor. I held myself in a tight ball and rocked back and forth, the pain making my entire body ache. I cannot believe how much this hurts.

We all grieve in different ways
And at different times
I will respect your grief
And you will respect mine
So that separately,
And together
We will heal…

February 14, 1995

You are my little Valentine, Cheyenne. I miss you so much. I want so desperately to hold you in my arms again. The time we had together was too brief. I wish I could have just a few more minutes to hold you again. It is not fair to wait so long for someone you love so much, only to have to say goodbye.

I would give anything for more time with you. Time to make a few more memories, which I can cherish. Time to tell you how much I love you. My body, my mind, my spirit and my heart ache for you. It just hurts so intensely.

I brought you some big heart balloons and red and pink roses. There was a new baby buried close to you at the cemetery. I cried for hours. Someone bought me a book called "On Children and Death," written by a woman psychiatrist, Dr. Kubler-Ross. She worked a lot with parents of children who died during or shortly after birth. It helped me so much. For the first time, I don't feel crazy for the emotions I am experiencing and the book validated everything, even the value of my child's life. Finally, someone heard me.

Grief is a strange emotion
One moment, quiet in a corner
The next erupting like an angry volcano
And yet,
Grief is good
I am thankful that I can grieve
That I can feel it in my soul
It heals me
It cleanses me
And it makes me strong
So I can face tomorrow...

If only for a moment
One more precious moment in time...

The time we had was too brief
 I could not tell you all about the love in my heart for you,
And that my life will never be the same without you in it.

Another moment to feel
The gift of your beauty
And to caress your soft, downy hair
To wrap your tiny, perfect hand around my finger

Only one more moment
Just one cherished kiss on your warm, soft lips...
One more tender stroke against your pink, rosy cheek
I would hold you tight
Close to my aching heart...
My falling tears a token of my forever love
One more moment to memorize every feature
Forever in awe of your beautiful innocence

Just a fraction of time
I held you in my arms
Yet from now until eternity
You will be mine...

March 4, 1995

Arman and I were at Grandma's house today. Arman was sitting at the kitchen table eating cereal. I was in the living room with Nana. Suddenly, there was a massive explosion in the kitchen. Nana and I screamed and ran into the kitchen where Arman was eating.

The large television had exploded and there were huge spears of glass everywhere. I panicked and carefully stepped through the destruction to get to Arman. He sat, about four feet from the television that had just exploded, very still and quiet at the table, large spears of thick glass all around. I began to cry as I grabbed him. We moved him into the living room and searched his body for glass. I had expected several injuries or cuts to his body. I was very surprised when we realized that not one piece of glass had touched him.

It was incredible. We looked at the area where he sat. Thousands of pieces of glass were scattered within inches of him and not one scratch on him.

I am so thankful that Arman wasn't hurt today. Sometimes I wonder if somehow you are able to take care of us from where you are, like a guardian angel.

One thing is sure, your life and death has given me a deeper appreciation for my other children. I am no longer naïve. I have lost my innocence. I am certain that the death of a child is the most difficult of all grieving processes to go through. I do not ever want to go through this again.

Since your death, I have come to know myself like never before. I never imagined I had so many different emotions buried within my soul. I will never take a moment in life for granted. I will cherish each and every day and be thankful for every second I have with my three beautiful children.

Even though we are absent
One from another
I will grow in my love for you
I will grow in my understanding of you
I will grow within myself because of you...

April 6, 1995

You aren't going to believe this, Cheyenne. Remember that counselor I visited last November? Well, he called me this evening at 6:30 p.m. He had a quiver in his voice. I knew something was wrong, terribly wrong. He and his wife lost their little girl during labor last week. She was born still.

I could not believe it! I stayed with him on the phone for about thirty minutes and we cried together. He said he was so glad he had the opportunity to meet me last year. He it prepared him for handling the shock and the early grief he was now experiencing.

He and his wife started a baby's book and took a lot of pictures of their daughter. He also apologized and said that he felt God brought us together to teach him something.

I went down to his office later that evening and we visited for awhile. We talked about his daughter and her birth. We also got a chance to talk about you and the errors he had made during our initial counseling session. This degree of grief is certainly not something you can learn at a university or in a book. I appreciated his validation.

Some things in life
We cannot see or understand
But certainly God will bring us
To others who can help
And then in return, we can help another

He does not take away
He restores...

April 20, 1995

I am here in the children's room watching them sleep. It reminds me of when they were babies. They are beautiful and I love them so much. Just like I love you, Cheyenne.

I don't think I have ever taken my children for granted, but it is so easy to take the time we have together for granted. I always assumed that I would wake up each morning and that they would be here. I used to feel secure that each time I kissed them goodbye as they went to school that they would return home at the end of the day. It's not that simple anymore.

Now I know. The death of a child can happen to anyone, anywhere, anytime. No one is exempt. I make a conscious effort to appreciate every moment. It is a gift to be able to look into their eyes and tell them how much they mean to me. It is a simple part of life that was stolen from me when you died.

So now I know that every moment I have with my children might be the last. It is a harsh reality. Perhaps that is why people do not want to talk about the death of a child, avoiding the subject at all costs. Maybe it is because they do not want to think that it could ever happen to them. It is painful to even think about. It is every parent's worse nightmare.

Tragedy will break you
Or it can rebuild you
You can become ashes and dust
Or a tower of fortitude
The broken spirit
Can evolve into a mighty one
All it needs is hope, faith, courage, love
And remembrance ~
You can never forget

My Sweetest One

In appreciation of Arman and Cameron, my beautiful sons
Written December 12, 1988,
Arman then 2 years old, Cameron then four months old

My Sweetest Ones-
There are many miracles of life and environment.
The certainty of a picturesque sunrise each dawn,
The vast bodies of water which encompass the earth
       And support the unquestionable cycle of life.

My Sweetest Ones-
Soon you will wonder at it all.

Miracles of the limitless varieties of life.
Colors of the distinct seasons,
Aromas of crimson-petal flowers.
The miraculous transformation of a simple caterpillar
       Into an exquisite, honey-sipping butterfly.

But You, My Sweetest Ones-
You are the most precious of life's miracles.

As I watch you when you sleep,
I feel a tender warmth in my heart.
As you gaze bewilderingly into my eyes
I find it hard to comprehend this overwhelming love
I hold for only you
A love that knows no boundaries or limitations

You, My Sweetest Ones,
I will cherish and love you forever.

You are my sons,
You are my miracles...

May 11, 1995

Your death has made me so much more spiritual, Cheyenne. I used to doubt the existence of God. Now I know that I have been carried through the past year and that you continue to touch my life in miraculous ways.

Yet, I still have so many lingering questions. I don't understand why so many innocent children die. I read that more than 30,000 babies a year are stillborn in America: Another 2,500 babies die as Sudden Infant Death Syndrome (SIDS) cases, and 17,000 babies die in the first 28 days of life. Thousands and thousands more die in car accidents, fires, and drownings. I am sure God understands why I question issues like this. So many families are crushed with grief; it just doesn't make sense. I don't feel guilty for my doubts and questions though. He created us all, so He completely comprehends our bewilderment.

I keep reliving the words that "God has a plan for me..." I cannot accept that a God of love would ever take a child away, as so many would have me believe, but I do trust that this type of tragedy will bring a person into a spiritual dimension that transcends our mere humanity. There has been an awakening in my soul since your death. And I believe that only God could have brought me to this place, for I would never have found it on my own.

I wonder if you will still be a little girl when we meet again in Heaven?

Sometimes I cannot wait
Until I pass to the other side
I know you are waiting for me
With your arms open
Ready to embrace me
My hearts quivers when I think about that moment
When I can once again hold you
On the other side

When We Meet Again

How will I know you?

Will it really ever be
that I can hold you in my arms
After holding you in my heart
for so long?

Will you whisper my name
"Mommy"
In the sweet voice of a little girl?
Or will you cry out like an angelic orchestra
in glorious awakening?

Will you wrap your tiny arms around my neck?
If you do,
I will never let you go.

I am sure I will know you
When our eyes meet
My spirit will recognize your s
And we will dance together, you and I

Will you tell me
That you've missed me
As much as I have you?
That it's been you all along
Protecting and caring for us?

Surely, I will know you
When we meet again.
Because fifty years from now
You will still be my little girl.

June 21, 1995

Tomorrow is Stevie Jo's birthday. We stopped by Grandma's house with her, Cameron and Arman. Even though it is Stevie Jo's birthday, Nana bought presents for all three children.

As we left, we loaded all the new toys into the car. The boys got into the back and Stevie Jo sat up front with me. I reached across her to seat belt her in. Grandpa and Nana were standing on her side of the car, waving goodbye. As I reached across to close Stevie Jo's door, I also locked it. Grabbing the handle, I began to pull it shut. As I did, she put her hand outside the door to reach Grandpa for another hug.

The door shut tight with her hand completely caught! I screamed and panicked. I struggled to quickly unlock the door so I could free her. Grandpa was also trying to open the door from the outside, making unlocking the door more difficult. Unable to unlock it, I tried to pull her hand out. It was stuck tight.

Stevie Jo began to cry hysterically. What seemed like hours was actually only seconds; we got the door open. I was sure she would have five broken fingers, and possibly a broken wrist.

I grabbed her hand now crying along with her. As I examined her, she stopped crying. We could not believe it when we discovered that there was not even a red mark anywhere on her hand or wrist. She did not have one mark, bruise or cut anywhere! I wriggled her wrist and each finger in disbelief. Nothing hurt her, anywhere!

Thank you, my little miracle.

Like the gentle, unseen breeze
The presence of those loved and lost
Remains with us always
I Remember
I believe

July 20, 1995

I contacted Phoenix Children's Hospital today. Your birthday is coming up and I wanted to plan something special for a needy family in your memory.

The social worker gave me the name and number of a family that desperately needed help. This afternoon, I met Christina, a 23-year-old woman with five children and little money. I called her and offered her some help with back to school shopping for her children. I explained why I wanted to help her and that your first birthday was coming. I told her that you were not here with us and that it would make me happy if I could spend the money I would have used for your birthday to help her children.

She graciously accepted my invitation. I went to her home and picked them all up. Her children were wonderful, Cheyenne. They were very excited and obviously thankful even before we departed for the shopping spree. We were all hungry so first we went to dinner. What beautiful children she has! We shopped for a few hours. They were very happy to receive new clothes and shoes. It was a very nice feeling to be able to help.

I have also organized a toy drive at work. It ends July 25th, just in time for your birthday. I will donate the toys and clothes to Lincoln Learning Center again. The response seems to be going very well. A lot of people are donating nice things for the children at the center.

There is a blessing
Even in the smallest of gifts
For kindness and compassion
Heals the heart
Touches the mind
And empowers the spirit

July 25, 1995

It is the end of the toy drive today. We brought two trucks full of new clothes and toys for the children at Lincoln Learning Center. It is bittersweet.

I wish you were here, Cheyenne, so I could spend your first birthday with you. I can't write anymore, my head feels so cloudy. I still cannot believe you are not here with us. I miss you and I love you. It will be your birthday in two days, and you belong here with your family.

It just isn't fair. I feel like I am falling apart. God, please help me get through the next few days. Help me to remember her beauty with joy and appreciation. Help me to look forward to the future, when we will be reunited. Help me to appreciate the gifts she has left for me. Help me to trust in the promise of eternal life.

One day at a time
Is all I can bear
If I can make it through this day
Then I can look back tomorrow
And know that I am strong
Even in my weakness
And sometimes being weak
Is the only way
That I can be
at all...

July 27, 1995

Happy Birthday, Sweetheart   .
It has been one long year since your death.

I wonder if you are there now with your first friends
Timmy, Matthew, Justin, and Caitlin...?

They say we've made it through
                    The first of times
                              The worst of times.

Our first hello...our first good-bye
Our first tears...that first desperate grief
Never willing to accept this as reality
Knowing that we will soon awaken to your hungry cries.

Our first Thanksgiving Day Prayers
Sitting in silence with tear filled eyes
                    Unable to speak a word
Still thankful for what we have
                    But overwhelmed by what we have lost.

Our first Christmas Day Celebration
It can never again be as joyous or complete
For just as in our hearts
                    Your places around our trees will be forever vacant

My first Mother's Day
Longing to spend a day at the park with all of my children together.
Longing to hear your giggling voices
                    Echoing across the playground.

Wondering what you would have sounded like
                    looked like
                              felt like

And now, for me, I am faced with your first birthday.
The others have survived this day, but will I?

No pictures of your first steps...your first smiles...

Your first messy bite
of a sweet ripened peach.
No first birthday candle...on your first birthday cake.
It has been one very long year since your death.

But if you are there with your first friends,
                    Tell me are you happy?

Did you share with them your first song...your first dance?
        Your first celebration of the other side?

Tell them we have survived the first of times
        the worst of times.

Surviving it by knowing that we will again be reunited.
And that the next time
        we are in each other's arms
           will be for eternity.

Dedicated to the families of Timmy, Matthew, Justin and Caitlin and their parents, my friends in grief: Julie, Dean, Heather, and Kim. And dedicated to our children who have crossed to the other side, together.

August 7, 1995

Your big sister, Stevie Jo, is an amazing child! Today was a particularly hard day for me. I wanted to cry all day, but was too busy. Postponing the grief only seems to make it worse.

Sensing my anguish, Stevie Jo took me into her room and hugged me. She told me that she missed you and asked if I missed you too. She opened her heart to me and encouraged me to talk about you and what you would have been doing. I told her that you'd probably be walking now and that she'd be able to chase you around the house. It made us both laugh.

But we cried together, too, realizing that you will not be here for those times. It is amazing to me that a child so young is brave enough to share these painful memories with me. It means so much. Just her smile warms my heart in my darkest moments. She would have been a wonderful sister to you, Cheyenne.

I am so thankful for her. When no one else wants to share the tears and no one else will really talk to me, Stevie Jo is there to offer a hug and a kind word. She was the best gift Heaven could have sent.

Give your children all of your love
Share with them
Your deepest emotions
The good and the bad
Give freely to your children
And they will give freely back to you.

For Stevie Jo...my angel on earth...

When you look into my eyes
In that very moment, little girl
I realize I cannot hide the pain and emptiness from you
You gently wipe piercing tears from my cheek
And with your heart, you share with me the memory
Of your sister...As no one else dares to do.

It is then, little girl...
That very moment
When I realize...
You are special, wise beyond your years
You are an enormous shining light...Heaven sent...to my life.
No, you are not so little at all.
        You Are Very, Very Big.

October 23, 1995

We bought a new home, Cheyenne! It is beautiful, in a wonderful neighborhood. They are building it now and we should be moving in December. The children will be in the best school district in the state.

But I will have to take down your nursery when we move. I cannot imagine how difficult it will be. It has remained untouched since your death. Sometimes I sit in there late at night and imagine what it would have been like to see you sleeping peacefully in your crib- or playing with all of your toys.

I have gone on with my life, even though some days, I wish I didn't have to. But I am still here and I am a survivor. Nevertheless, there is always something missing. It never feels quite complete. It can never feel complete without you.

I visited the home-site today. As I walked through our half-constructed house, my thoughts were consumed with how perfect it would be to have you here with us. I had visions of you living here with us. I rewound the tape of your birth and death again and changed the outcome in my mind. You'd have your own room here, across from Stevie Jo's. Of course, I'd have to use safety gates on both sets of stairs and child proof the cabinets.

My dreams of you make me smile. So for now, I'll keep on dreaming.

Thinking of you
Fills my heart with gladness
Thinking of you
Fills my heart with pain
I would not trade
That gladness or that pain
For anything in the world
Except to have you back again...

The Mask

I feel as if I am buried alive
Yet I smile, and respond
"Fine, thank you."
I have been appropriately conditioned
No one wants to hear the painful
t   r   u   t   h

A part of me, like a phantom limb
A constituent of my earthly being
Has been violently amputated.
Yet I try to laugh at the mediocre conversations
A verbal splash in a shallow puddle
Pretending to be a player of the words
That have no
m   e   a   n   i   n   g

My heart has been ripped open
No benevolence granted
No explanation - No apologies
Only cataclysmic
p   a   i   n
No anesthesia remains, just the bitter pain.

Yet I wear the mask.

Sequestered, as they remain
Unconscious of
my words, my pain
The indigenous language of my sad
e   y   e   s

They will never really know me,
It's only a mask.

November 16, 1995

It is time for another birthday, Cheyenne. I am 30 years old. Some days it doesn't seem to be getting any easier. It just seems that day-by-day I manufacture another piece of camouflage to lay over my bleeding heart.

I went to the cemetery tonight. I tended to your grave (& Timmy's too) and then began to head towards the car. In the distance, I could see someone at the other end of the cemetery. Something was drawing me towards her. With mascara running down my face, however, I didn't want to meet anyone. I ignored that unrelenting urge to go toward her.

The feeling persisted all the way to the car. As I tried to hurry away, I heard a voice cry out to me. It was the woman I had been trying to avoid. I started walking to meet her, thinking she may need my help. As we neared each other, I noticed she was an older woman, about 65-years old, who had been crying. Without saying a word, we embraced each other and cried. Her name was Mathilda. For the next thirty minutes, she proceeded to tell me about her 45-year marriage to Victor. She told me about his recent death. I listened sympathetically, to her story.

She mentioned that Victor knew he was going to die. She said that for three days before his death he kept seeing a little girl outside his window. The little girl was urging him to follow her. He saw the little girl several times. Mathilda told Victor that she could not see the little girl, and she asked him to describe her. He responded, "She is **too beautiful**, and words cannot describe her."

Mathilda asked me if I was visiting a relative at the cemetery. That is when I told her that my daughter had passed away. She was silent for a moment. Then she asked, "Do you suppose it was your little girl Victor saw?" I responded, "Anything is possible with angels."

I did not tell Mathilda but on your grave, is the inscription:

"Cheyenne Cacciatore, July 27, 1994
Precious daughter .... Too beautiful for this world"

December 5, 1995

I read a quote today which I really loved. It says,

"Have you come to that Red Sea place in your life...where there is no way out and no way back. The only way is through."

That's where I stand with this pain. I must move through it. I recognize the validity of all my emotions, regardless what people whisper behind my back. I hear them questioning my grief. I see them stare at me with unsettled eyes. I see them analyzing each word relating to your death. They think I am "not okay" because I cry. They think I am wallowing in grief. They think I am taking it too far. They are so wrong. They don't even have a clue! I know who I am and what I am doing! I am going "through" the grief. I am not hiding from the pain. I am not pretending it didn't happen. I won't let them force me to withdraw from the reality of your death. I am living the experience. It takes a lot more strength to face it then to run from it. I am strong- I am!

Creator of the universe
Keeper of the Stars
Guardian of the Heavens
Look within my heart
Search the depths of my spirit
Comfort my aching heart
For you are also
Creator of Her soul
Keeper of her spirit
Guardian of my child

December 24, 1995

I am certain the holidays are the most difficult. Everyone is so happy. No one seems to remember that I am *still* grieving and no one *really* wants to talk about you except the wonderful people at Compassionate Friends. We all hold an understanding that it is a bittersweet season. Some people may think that talking about our child brings pain. The truth is, not talking about it hurts much worse. Others who have been through this understand that talking about children who have died is a natural and healthy desire for parents.

I was thinking about how wonderful and amazing it would be to have you here with us. What kinds of toys would you have asked for? Our Christmas cards this year were very special. I have decided that somehow, every year, I will include you in them. So, this year to honor this new tradition, our cards read:

"To celebrate in a world full of pain means you must believe in hope. We take this time to cherish and remember our pr ecious daughter and sister, Cheyenne and the many priceless gifts she has left us. Take this time to cherish those you love. In Memory of Cheyenne, July 27, 1994."

You are part of our family and always will be. I won't let anyone forget you.

I went to the cemetery to decorate. I bought you a beautiful purple candle to light and a huge angel flag. I cried and cried and cried. This festive time of year feels so uncomfortable. I want you here with us. My arms still ache for you. I left at dusk, your candle burning in the winter wind.

Amidst the laughter and celebration
I will turn my head away
And cry tears of sadness
For I remember the missing piece
That cannot be replaced
With gifts and festivities
I remember you with love
Even when others don't.

Dear God,

Can you hear me?
Please, God. Do you hear my cries?
The ones that echo pain deep within my mind and heart.

She is gone, God. My little girl is dead.
And I love her so.
I've tried to pray
              To seek
                    To beg

And still, she is gone.
I would have given my life for hers...

I do not understand.
You see, God, she left so suddenly.
Without saying good-bye
                  Or even hello.

How can it be that she has changed my life so?
How can it be that others think I should forget her so abruptly
      And go on with my life?

How can I pretend that she did not exist?

For her life and death have brought me on my knees to You.
And now I seek the peace which only Your midst can harbor
To ease this overwhelming grief.

But still God, I feel cheated.

I feel so very desperate for her presence.

I never looked into her eyes
        I never told her how much she meant to me
                Or how much her mother loved her.

But you can God.
Please, please
        tell her for me.
For I know she is in Your care.

Tell her that her beauty has left me many priceless gifts.
Tell her that I think of her
        Every day, every hour, every moment.

Tell her how deeply I love and miss her, that I will never forget her,
        And that the world will know of the little girl who died.

Hold her in Your majestic arms, just for me, Lord.

Rock her gently and whisper in her ear
Tell her that her mommy aches for her, still and always.

For the only strength that remains is the strength which You grant me

In knowing that You, and only You,
Can love her the way that I do...

Amen

January 9, 1996

It has been sixteen days since my visit to the cemetery on Christmas Eve. I brought your brothers and sister with me today, and I have been given a miraculous gift of faith!

As we arrived at your grave and began to tend to it, I looked at the candle I had bought you for Christmas. Remarkably, the candle I had lit sixteen days earlier on Christmas Eve was still burning with no wax left in the candle at all. All that remained was a tiny wick and flame.

We were amazed! I tried to rationalize how that could have occurred (you know how analytical I am). It had rained between Christmas Eve and today. And with the wind, the sprinklers, and a sixteen-day time span, it seemed impossible. I had to accept it as a gift. I fell to my knees and began to cry.

It was then that I realized that you were whispering to me. I was given the gift of reassurance. Just as the candle was still burning, I was reassured that your life continued. God has given you eternal life and He has given me the promise of a reunion.

My faith and the hope
That I will see you again
Will sustain me.
Faith that one glorious day
I will awaken with you in my arms.

Resolutions

Another Year
Time passes so quickly.

A new home,
new job,
new friends,
new school.
The New Year
        and the new promises it holds.

So many changes
Since July of '94

But some things never change.

Even though
My life goes on
Even though
The tears don't come everyday
Even though it seems
My heart has finally begun to heal
Even though
18 months have passed since your death

There are things which the sands of time will never change

No matter where I am
No matter what I do
No matter how much time passes
No matter who I grow to become

I will always be your mother
You will always be my daughter
And I will always love you.

February 3, 1996

My new neighbor, Jami, and I have become very close. Her mother died when she was a teenager. She seems to sympathize with my pain. I appreciate that she never attempts to say the right things, but often when I feel sad, she will just listen.

We went to the cemetery today. Jami was the first person, besides me, to visit you. After sitting by your grave for awhile, we went over to visit Timmy. He had a very old Mylar balloon knotted up around the windmills that Heather had placed on his grave. As I struggled to untangle the mess, I told Jami about Timmy and how I met his mother at Compassionate Friends. The balloon was deflated and was so old that the silver was peeling off and getting all over my hands and clothing.

I told Jami about Timmy's passion as a two-year-old boy to fly like Peter Pan. As I freed the balloon, I laid it on the ground for a moment to trim the grass around his headstone. We headed for the trash; one of my hands filled with grass the other holding the balloon. I threw the grass away and then put the flattened balloon into the garbage. We continued to talk about you and Timmy. And then I saw Jami's mouth drop open and her eyes become huge. I turned to look. The balloon I had just put into the trash lifted out of the garbage and, like a balloon newly filled with helium, it drifted deep into the blue sky.

Jami and I stood there staring in silent reverence until the balloon was completely out of sight.

I tell myself
Quiet, please, mind
Silence, please, my spirit
I want to hear
I want to listen
If I open my heart
I will hear the answers

March 15, 1996

Stevie Jo asked me if I would ever have another child today and if I did, she wondered if the new child would be you. I tried to explain to her that you could never be replaced. Then the boys started asking a lot of questions about you. They admitted that they resented the fact that they never got to say goodbye to 'their baby sister.' They expressed that they had wanted to be there at the hospital and the mortuary with us. I apologized to them realizing that I made a terrible mistake. In retrospect, I recall questioning my judgment when we excluded them from the funeral. I should have offered them the opportunity to hold and get to know their sister. I asked them to forgive me and said that I was trying to protect them. They hugged me and I cried.

It has been twenty months since your death. It seems the time in between the waves of grief gets a little longer and easier to deal with. The grief no longer consumes every move I make and every thought I think. But God, I miss you so much.

Many days have passed
Since I touched your face
Many hours have passed
Since I kissed your lips
But I can still feel you, I can still smell you
Your presence remains with me
Everyday, every moment.
I love you.

May 1, 1996

I found out yesterday that I am pregnant, Cheyenne! I am excited that I will soon have your brother or sister. But I am ambivalent about many things too. So many questions are running through my mind. Is it a boy or girl? Will he or she look like you? When will he or she be born? But I am afraid too. I cannot imagine enduring another death.

Stevie Jo is the most excited in the family. Every morning she kisses my tiny belly when I drop her off at school. She doesn't let me leave her without saying goodbye to the baby. Sometimes she asks if the baby is going to die but I try to reassure her. For the most part, she is very comfortable with it. Arman and Cameron are excited too! I think they are confused by my varying emotions. Sometimes I am elated and floating on air and other times I cannot bear the emotional stress and break down in tears.

I don't miss you any less today than I did the day you died. I am just surviving day-to-day knowing that when this child is born we will have a little piece of you in our home to love and cherish. I am considered a high-risk pregnancy so they are taking appropriate precautions to make sure everything goes well. Dr. Novick assures me that the chance of this happening again, particularly when there was no medical explanation for your death, is very low. When I am being realistic, I feel comforted by those statistics.

We went to see Julie and her new baby, Chase. He is beautiful. I went to the florist to pick out an arrangement for them. The emotions hit when I saw all the "It's a girl" balloons and ceramic pink booties. I spent most of the visit with them sharing tears of happiness and sorrow. I think Julie felt the same way. Chase doesn't replace Caitlin for her and his presence doesn't lessen the pain. It is just a new beautiful person to love and care for.

The light is here
I think I have reached it
Sometimes I go back into the darkness
And the pain returns like a flood
But most often these days I linger in the light
Where I can cherish you
And see you clearly in the light

Beginnings

A new baby is on the way.

Not just any baby.
It is your little brother or sister.
A part of you.

I am so afraid,
    and excited
            and angry
                and sad.

Afraid of being hurt again
Excited that I will have another child,
to give my love to

Angry that you are gone
And sad,
Every moment wishing you were here with us.

All of these emotions
Sometimes make me feel crazy.

But I know I am not.
I am just a grieving mother

Missing what should have been.

June 6, 1996

The pregnancy is going well. My attitude is very good most of the time. Occasionally, I feel a little neurotic. I fear having to go through the death of another child. I know in my heart everything will be fine, but once you are struck by lightning, you tend to cringe at the hint of a coming storm.

I am seeing the psychologist every other month. He helps me handle the incessant nightmares I've been having. I dream that this baby dies. It is horrible. He assures me that all these feelings are quite normal and that he would be surprised if I was feeling anything different. He recommended visual imagery to assist me in relaxing after the nightmares. I have to pick a beautiful place where I would love to be and put myself there. The first time I tried the imagery, I chose to visualize being in Sedona near the stream. But last night, when I had a nightmare, I brought myself to your arms. It was beautiful. I knew it was not real but it felt wonderful to pretend myself there, even for a brief time.

People at the office have found out about the pregnancy. Some seem to think that this will "make my pain all better." It frustrates me. If my mother or father died, people would not expect me to "replace" them or encourage me to take their pictures down. Why is it they expect that when your child dies?

Their only excuse is their ignorance. I am glad they are ignorant, for I wouldn't wish this journey on anyone.

Teach me to love others
Through compassion and appreciation
Teach me to guide them
With love and acceptance
Teach me to understand them
With patience and kindness

Why can't they understand?
If I become blind
In one of my eyes
Of course I am still grateful
For the vision that remains in the other.

But I will never stop mourning the absence
Of my precious eye
The one which I lost

My vision is changed forever

I will never, ever
See things the same again.

July 1, 1996

Feeling pretty sarcastic about life today. I do not like the month of July. I want to take it off the calendar. The sequence could be: May, June, then August and September. It is too hot in July anyway and that would cut the length of our unbearable summers down. At least I have a bit of humor left.

Your second birthday is coming up. Attempting to monopolize my thoughts and channel the upcoming sadness, I organized another toy drive for the Lincoln Learning Center. We will distribute the toys at the end of the month.

It is hard to believe that nearly two years have passed since your birth and death. I am such a different person. Sometimes I surprise myself with the bold things I say and do.

Today someone at work noticed my pictures. She asked about the children's ages and specifically inquired about you. I tried to avoid the subject by replying, "Their ages range from four to nine," however, she persisted with the questioning. Unable to circumvent the topic, I told her about you. She replied that God probably needed 'another angel in heaven to tend His garden'. I told her that was ridiculous. God would never be so cruel as to give a child to me simply to take the child away. As we continued to talk about dealing with the death of a child, I discovered that her sister's little girl recently died.

I gave her some information on Compassionate Friends and some tips on helping and supporting her sister. I am hopeful that, one by one, people will begin to become more sensitive to the needs of bereaved parents as awareness begins to spread.

I am at a place now
A beautiful place
Where I can help others
And teach others
And give to others
Touching lives
All for you
All because of you...

Terrible Two's

If you were here
We'd be celebrating
As you turned two

A big girl now!
Maybe you'd be potty trained?
Pulling books off shelves
Clothes out of drawers
Splashing water on my newly cleaned windows!
Even chocolate pudding on the floor.

Falling deep asleep
In my arms
On a stormy monsoon night.

Wouldn't it be heaven
In our home
If you were here?

July 27, 1996

Dear Cheyenne,

Here I am kneeling at your grave. You would have been two-years-old today. I should be getting ready for your party...blowing up balloons, decorating the house, making cupcakes, wrapping all your presents (you would have been spoiled just like the other three).

But here I kneel, at your little plot of grass, my heart aching, tears flowing from my eyes. I am in so much pain that I cannot stand up. I brought you the less traditional birthday gifts.... four Mylar balloons, twelve pink roses (we brought thirteen, but one is for Victor at the cemetery) and candles which manage to stay lit through the windy eve.

We came to say Happy Birthday, Cheyenne. So we hold hands in a circle around your grave and sing to you- Arman, Cameron, Stevie Jo, your unborn baby brother, and I.

Looking at my bulging belly, I realize this next child will be a very special child. I am thankful for the chance to care for and love your little brother. I will dedicate my heart and my life to this baby, just as I have dedicated my life to caring for Arman, Cameron, and Stevie Jo.

But today, I also dedicate my life to you too, Cheyenne. I cannot care for your physical being, but my heart, my spirit, and my mind will carefully tend your memory forever. I will never forget you. Nor will I even try. I only want to love you, to cherish you, and to anticipate the day when we will spend eternity together in each other's arms. That hope and my faith will make this birthday and each birthday to come more tolerable.

I love you forever, my littlest angel.

Yours forever,
Mommy

August 1, 1996

After much deliberation, I made the decision to start a group called Mothers in Sympathy and Support. My dreams are coming to fruition. The acronym for the group is MISS. I chose it because we all *miss* our children so much. We will offer workshops on grief education for hospitals, funeral homes, and first responders. We will also offer one-on-one support for parents after the death of a child.

I know it will be disheartening to immerse myself in death, but it is the only way I can make sense of this horrible tragedy. I really want to help professionals understand how to help families emotionally through the death of a child. They need to understand the families' needs for ritual, compassion, and end of life care. They need to encourage families to hold their child and say goodbye. They need to know what options to offer family members and *how* to offer them. I should have the training overview completed by next week. Hopefully, we will be ready for the workshops in several weeks.

The new baby is due in four months. I am feeling more and more anxious. Thankfully, Dr. Novick has been wonderful. He addresses all my concerns and doesn't treat me like a paranoid pregnant woman. He answers all my questions and really helps me feel comfortable. I don't know if I could do this without his help. Next week I am attending the first baby shower since you died. I think I will be okay. I am just holding my breath and waiting.

Can it be
So much time has passed
That I am now comfortable
In the presence of glowing pregnant women
And beautiful infant girls?
Can it be
Time has done its job?

September 18, 1996

I may not be as strong as I thought; I am still on that roller coaster ride. There was a huge company picnic today. It was really nice and hundreds of people were there. While the kids were playing Frisbee, I suddenly saw them- the couple who had their little girl in August of 1994, one week after you died.

The mother was holding one of her hands and the father was holding the other. They were coming toward the picnic from across the parking lot. I began to shake. I was looking at what I should have: A beautiful, ebony-haired two-year-old girl in pink corduroy overalls, holding her parents' hands. I stared at them. Tears welled up in my eyes. I knew that I was not going to be able to handle it. That is what *our* family should have looked like.

Knowing the outburst erupting, I got the kids together and ready to leave. I was dazed and paralyzed. We left the picnic without saying goodbye to anyone. I couldn't face people. The rest of the day was melancholy for all of us. I miss you so much.

Where is the justice in death?
Who chooses the ones that stay?
And those who don't?
Let me ask Him
The myriad of questions
Beginning with,
Why me?

September 22, 1996

Today is the Sibling Childbirth Preparation Class Day. I decided to have the children present for Joshua Cheyne's birth in December so I signed all the kids up for this class. I really want them to witness the miracle of his birth and to share that special event with me. I am sure it will change their lives forever to watch their baby brother come into this world. So off to the class we all went.

All the pregnant women came to the class with their children. But I felt so out of place. I was not like them; I have been to hell and back. I could tell it was going to be a rough day for me from the start. Then, halfway through the class, the woman sitting next to us with her two-year-old daughter said, "Cheyenne, come back here."

I dropped my head down trying to cover my eyes with my long hair. I didn't want to talk about you there, Cheyenne. I didn't want to scare all those women. I excused myself and went to the bathroom where I hid for the rest of the class. Hearing your name was such a shock for me.

I have taken a hiatus as leader of the infant group for Compassionate Friends. I need to concentrate on getting through the rest of this pregnancy and maintaining my sanity.

I am not alone
I cannot be alone
I know You would never leave me
I know
Without doubt
That
I am in divine company

December 12, 1996

Dear Cheyenne,

At 2:12 p.m., I gave birth to your baby brother, Joshua Cheyne (pronounced Shane) Cacciatore. He was named after you. What a bittersweet day! Your brothers and sister, Nana and Papa, Kelly, and Jami were all there to welcome him, and to help me.

As my labor progressed, I became very emotional. I had not prepared for the upheaval of my heart. For two hours, as I labored during the birth of your brother, I cried uncontrollably. I brought your picture to the hospital so you could be here with us. Sobbing with the fear of losing our precious new child, and sobbing with the pain that you are not here with us to welcome him into our lives, the stress was unbearable.

Then when your brother's head crowned, the nurse said, "Look at his dark curly hair," I really lost control. He was born seconds later with hair just like yours. In fact, he looked exactly like you did the day that you were born. It was a combination of overwhelming joy and overwhelming sorrow. I was so relieved I had a healthy son, yet it made me miss you even more. Your brother weighed seven pounds, three ounces. He was two weeks early, born on your oldest brother, Arman's, 10th birthday. He truly is a special baby.

I promise you, Cheyenne, one day your baby brother will know all about his beautiful and special sister. We will always remember you.

I love you, Cheyenne,

Mommy

January 2, 1997

This is the second most difficult day of my life. My friends, Todd and Gina, lost their second child, Nicholas. They asked me to come and meet Nicholas before he died. I did. It was horrible. I could barely control my own tears or bring myself to look into the emptiness in Todd or Gina's eyes.

Joshua is two weeks old now. But their little son, the boy who was supposed to be Joshua's playmate, will never live to see two weeks. I don't understand. I just don't understand. The tears won't stop. I am going to the cemetery now.

Some people say
God won't give you more than you can handle
Easy for them to say
When they tuck their child
Into a warm, safe bed
Late at night...

Saving Nicholas

For my friends, Todd & Gina and for Nicholas, Courtney, and Miranda

Modern man
Can explore the extraterrestrials
He can clone and create new limbs
Unearth enigmas of the Amazon
Transmit signals across continents
To foreign lands and peoples

He can fertilize life inside a tube

But I watched in horror that day
January 2, 1997
When he was born
Small, frail child
Each subtle breath a marathon effort

His father
Helplessly looking on
Pupils dilated with contradiction
Baptized with tears
Holding his son, kissing him

Wanting to relinquish his own breath
To save his son

His mother
Donned in the robe of the holy
As a formality for the inevitable
She was pale, deceived by her body (for the second time)

Her legs trembled as she reached
Her arms out to hold his dying body.

The medicine men
And women
Come in and out, slow motioned
Casual observers

Auditing,
Updating meaningless records and numbers
I felt helpless and angry -
Agony, defeat
As I watched his gallant struggle

Gasping for each breath
Wanting to scream down the septic hallways
"Save him! Someone come and save him!"

Bargaining with God to
Trade my thirty years for his life.

And I went home that night, sobbing
And I held my own healthy, living
Newborn son in my arms.

Cursing God, yet praising Him

Modern man can do many great things
But he could not save Nicholas.

the perfect day.

the perfect day would be
          your aroma
filling every crevice of our home
inch by inch
               transcending the scent of french vanilla
               and huggies

the perfect day
          would be
awakening
in your quiescent embrace
as the leaves caress
      dew drops so reluctantly released
to a new days dawn

the perfect day would entertain
          evidence of your presence
around every corner
                    not just within the corners
                    of my mind

the perfect day would be
          a cherished goodnight kiss
and a Barney bear
          now i lay me and
sweet dreams

the perfect day would be
          canceling my contract
                    as a grieving parent
remiss of all this pain

the perfect day
          would be complete with you

January 3, 1997

It has been very busy around here, Cheyenne. Your baby brother is doing great and already weighs eleven pounds. He nurses every two hours, even all night. He sleeps with me and I never let him out of sight. I am tired, but I will never complain. I will take sleepless nights over the alternative any day.

The MISS group is growing rapidly. Our workshops have received outstanding reviews by those who have attended. We have even received accreditation for continuing education for nurses and funeral directors. We have come a long way, haven't we?

I have put in my resignation at work and have decided to stay home with Joshua. I cannot imagine leaving him with anyone. Hopefully, I will find a job I am able to do from my home office.

I have met a lot of wonderful people through MISS; people who have touched my life. We have been able to help nearly 100 families affected by the death of an infant. Most of the parents were referred to our group from local hospitals. The parents are so wonderful and receptive to our information. We will soon begin our own support group, specifically for infant death. I also went back to facilitating the Compassionate Friends meetings. It feels good to be back. I believe I have been called to this ministry.

I haven't been able to visit the cemetery more than once a month lately. It has been too busy around here and your baby brother hates the car.

You are still on my mind
You are still in my heart
You are still within my spirit
You are still my child, and my love

May 29, 1997

Time is flying by and I am staying really busy. I have presented workshops at more than seventy local hospitals, physicians' offices, funeral homes, and victim assistance programs for police and fire stations about grief and crisis intervention. I have also been a presenter at four National Conferences and will be a speaker at the upcoming Compassionate Friends conference in September. So many doors are opening!

We went to Disneyland last week. It was a long, long drive, but the kids had so much fun. You know, I was thinking about how my life is like a puzzle now. I can see the picture in the puzzle, it is clear and it is beautiful. But there is still a piece of the puzzle missing. It is never quite right without that piece. It can never be complete. And those darn Magic Kingdom signs screamed at me around every corner. I couldn't escape those signs. I am probably the only woman on earth who has cried at Disneyland.

May of '97
The sign said
"You must be at least
three years of age to ride."

We would have waited
Until July
To go to Disneyland

July 27, 1997

It is hard to believe that I have survived so long without you. You should be three-years-old today. I imagine the many mischievous things you'd do around the house. I picture you and Stevie Jo playing Barbie Dolls and house together. But that will never happen. The reality of your death is still like scalding water.

We went to the cemetery today and decorated with big Mylar balloons. The girl at the store asked if we were having a big party for our three-year-old. I told her it would be a quiet celebration at the cemetery. She looked like she swallowed her tongue. After we visited the cemetery, we left for a few days in New Mexico.

This year seems a little better for me. After three long years of no one acknowledging your birthday with a card or a call, I have broken the emotional barricade, at least with a few very special people. This year I received seven cards from friends who wanted to let me know that they remember and acknowledge your life. It was so wonderful! I cried with every card I opened. I can't express how much that meant to me. At the same time, I was saddened that some of the people who are closest to me still did not call or write. I don't know how to make them understand that I cannot and will not forget. I wonder if they have forgotten, and I struggle with anger and resentment even after three years.

Well, Cheyenne, I do silently celebrate your beautiful life today. I do remember your soft skin, your downy hair, and your tiny nose. I do cherish the memories, too few, but precious. (Your brother, Joshua reminds me so much of you. Sometimes when he sleeps, I can see your face in his.)

You are my gift, my angel. I am forever grateful that you came into my life. You are in my heart and I am in yours, always and forever.

An angel has passed
In the rippling of her wings, she touches our lives
Heavenward
Go little one, fly
We will never forget

Waiting

Never having known you the way I should have
Never having heard
Your sweet voice whispering my name in the night

Never expecting
This lonely battlefield.
Like a lone soldier, I fight a war I cannot win.

Never knowing you
The way every mother should know the flesh of her flesh

Others walk away and don't look back
They fear I will become that pillar of salt

But today on your 3rd birthday
I remember you
My beautiful daughter
The missing piece of our family

And I look forward to what I will have one day
When we are together
When I will know you again
And then we will celebrate
All the birthdays we have missed.

You are my special angel.

September 16, 1997

Jami helped me to create a web page on the Internet. It will help us get information to families about grief and surviving the death of a child. It is beautiful!

In just a few weeks, we have had more than three hundred visitors to the MISS web site! It's become so obvious to me that this type of support and information is desperately needed. I am working on another idea called the Kindness Project. Little cards which parents can leave anonymously whenever they perform an act of kindness in memory of their child. The card says, "*This random act of Kindness done in loving memory of our Beautiful Child (Child's Name here)."*

This Random Act of Kindness

Done in Loving Memory
of our Beautiful Child

_____

www.misschildren.org

It is an incentive for people to share the memory of their child by reaching out and helping another person. This card would have been great to leave at the Lincoln Learning Center for the toy drives. I didn't care if anyone knew me, but I did want them to know about you. I wanted them to know that you are so special and loved so much that your mommy is willing to reach out to others because of you.

Several news stations and newspapers have contacted me. They want to do a story on our group and the work that we do. The Kindness Project will certainly add some dimension to our work within the community. It reinforces the presence of goodness in the human spirit.

It is impossible to lift
The spirit and the life
Of another human being
Without also
Lifting the spirit
And the life
Of yourself
And your child

Small wonder
Simple faith
You are in each breath that I take

The simplicity of nature
The colorful wonders of life

Sunrise and sunset
And all the beauty and chaos between them

Not the mere words
But absolute language

You are more to me than just my child
You've given me wings
And you are the wind which carries me

Simple faith
Small wonder

October 26, 1997

The Kindness Project has been a huge success, Cheyenne! We have sold over 3,000 cards in less than one month! That represents 3,000 kind deeds being done. We have had orders from Texas, California, New Jersey, Pennsylvania, Florida, even Australia and Singapore. Bereaved parents, grandparents, siblings, aunts, and uncles are all participating. I am very pleased that it has been so successful. We expect to sell even more cards in the coming months for the holidays.

The weather has been spectacular! It is so nice to see it finally cooling off! We celebrated the reprieve from the heat by spending a glorious Sunday afternoon at the park followed by lunch at our favorite place, Mimi's Cafe. It is always interesting, to say the least, to watch the expression on people's faces as I walk in with four young children, diaper bag in tow, obvious looks of distress on our faces. They seated us in a booth (strategically placed in a corner) across from two elderly couples.

Lunch went as usual: Your baby brother, Joshua, now ten months old, crawling from sibling to sibling; grabbing glasses of water, spilling food synchronically with an occasional yelp. Your two older brothers were poking at each other and each other's food. Stevie Jo was admonishing the boys at every opportunity, giving them step by step instructions on probable chores they'd be performing when we got home as punishment for their incessant torturing of each other in public.

Attempting to maintain damage control, I concentrated on keeping voice levels down to a mild yell, oblivious to the existence of other human beings in the restaurant. After our meal was over, the older woman sitting across from us said, "What a beautiful family!" Startled that she wasn't annoyed by our presence, I said, "Thank you. We think they are beautiful too!" Noticing that Stevie Jo was the lone little girl of the family she said, "Too bad you only have one daughter. Are you going to try for another?"

Complete silence. I had a huge lump in my throat. What would I say? Would I agree? Would I tell her that I have two daughters? Would I deny you this day?

The children looked over at me, holding their breath, waiting for my reply. For the first time all afternoon, they were quiet. Even the baby knew something big was about to happen. Here was my opportunity to brandish my feelings about your death with a complete stranger. I responded with summoned confidence, "I do have another daughter, but she is in Heaven."

Silence again.

She smiled and went back to her meal. The obvious discomfort we all felt did not surprise me. I have felt that discomfort many times in the three years since your death. But as the elderly couples left the restaurant, the woman who had asked about our children approached our table. With kind, loving eyes she took my hand and said, " I am so very sorry about the death of your little girl. I can tell you are a good parent and that you love her very much." I was speechless, tongue-tied.

"Thank you, I am sorry too," I replied sheepishly.

She smiled and walked away.

I looked at the children and began to cry. That woman will never know how much the compassion she extended to me that day touched my heart. Her warmth and empathy reaffirmed my hopes that one-day, people will unite to support grieving parents, regardless of the age or cause of death of the child. That was her random act of kindness to me. It was a gift for which I will be eternally grateful.

A simple word or a touch
Can mean so very much
A shared moment or a thought
Take the time, rather than not

Death

Written February 27, 1985
Nine years before Cheyenne's death

Two seeds He plants with love
Are raised from Up Above,
The sun's sweet tender kiss
Will warm the winter's bliss.

Into One they shall become
From separate seeds apart,
To live, to breathe, to grow
Soon two become one heart.

Though time and circumstances know
The weathered fields and timeless flow,
Two seeds adjoin, embody one
The perfect life has just begun.

As one firm tree with roots of stone
Through weeds surrounding, daisies shone,
Stand tall and proud and in the Spring
Reap rich rewards that true love brings.

But the creatures in this forest fair
Now mourn and weep beyond their share,
The tree they love, so proud and strong
Now withers to the Piper's Song.

And echoes of the ones who cry
Tears fall like rain, and though we try,
To melt the winters ice that covers
The tree beneath the cold, now shudders.

(The daisies all have disappeared
   A solemn silence fills the air,
         That empty space none dares to fill
               The tree has died, and all is still.)

November 22, 1997

Last night I had a very profound dream involving another bereaved mom, Lois, whom I met on the Internet. Her daughter, Carol, died at age eleven. She and I have emailed each other a few times over the past several months. I had a dream that Carol was standing on a stage wearing a dark maroon velvet dress, with cream-colored lace around the collar. She was smiling a glorious smile and clapping her hands. Her aura was complete happiness and peacefulness. She looked very beautiful, like an angel. She asked me to tell her mother that she is doing well and that she loves her very much. The message was so clear that I could not ignore it.

I debated whether I should tell Lois. I have never had a dream like that before. It was one of those dreams that is so engrossing, I could not negate the message behind it. The decision to tell Carol's mom was difficult because I didn't want her to think I was crazy, nor did I want to upset her. Nevertheless, I was compelled to send her an email. I knew that if someone had such a profound and detailed dream about you, I would want to know. This is the response I received from her:

> *Dear Joanne,*
>
> *I am not upset at all! I thank you so much for sharing this with me. It means a lot to me. I close my eyes and see my little girl. She used to clap her hands and posture herself that way all the time. She would smile at people and just clap, clap, clap. Oh, the memories, they overwhelm me. By the way, Carol did have a velvet dark maroon, almost purple dress, with cream colored lace around the collar. I am touched that she was in your dreams looking out for her mommy.*
>
> *God bless you and Thank You!*
> *Carol's Mother*

December 18, 1997

Well, Cheyenne, your brother has made it to his first birthday on the 12th. It was bittersweet. I didn't forget that you should have been here with us to celebrate. I have been so busy. The web page has received over 4,500 visits from people worldwide. I receive email and letters everyday from families who appreciate the support. It makes all the work and dedication worthwhile.

The workshops are going very well and I am completely booked until the end of February. MISS has started its own support group and the response has been monumental. Nearly thirty people attended our November meeting. Timmy's (P. Pan) mom, Heather, was there. He is the oldest of the children in our group. Most of our parents have experienced early infant death. I am sad to see so many families endure this tragedy, however, I am so happy to know that they are being educated about our groups. No one should have to go through this nightmare alone.

I am getting ready for a Candlelight Memorial Service tonight. MISS families and Thunderbird Samaritan are organizing it. I am looking forward to a night of quiet, to remember and to celebrate your life.

Before we left for the candlelighting, your brother brought me your picture from the end table. He handed it to me. I told him, "That's Cheyenne, Joshua. She is your beautiful big sister in Heaven." He looked at me as if he knew what I was saying. He took your picture back from me and stared at you. I repeated what I had just told him about you. (As I promised, I will make sure he knows all about you). Then he took your picture, opened his mouth and kissed you. I was crying, as usual. But they were happy tears. I love you still and always will.

In his smile, I see your joy
In his laugh, I hear your happiness
In his walk, I see your beauty
In his eyes, I see your light

December 19, 1997

The candlelight service was incredible. The camaraderie in that room touched so many people. Something else amazing happened, Chey.

Jami volunteered to help us personalize the beautiful ornaments we ordered for the parents. She sat at a table in the back of the church while I sat in the front of the church. Jami called me this morning because she wanted to share something that happened. She said that at the end of the service, when the RTS coordinator from the hospital was thanking me, something wonderful happened: She said, "Thank you, Joanne. I know all that you do, you do because of Cheyenne." Jami said the star on the top of the Christmas tree, which had been unlit all night, suddenly lit up at the very moment she said your name. I got chills when she told me and felt envious that I had missed it. I thanked Jami for sharing it with me. It made me feel so good. I know you are always with me. I am so thankful for the confirmation.

Trust
Faith
Wisdom
Courage
Believe
Hope
Strength
Kindness
Remembrance
Each is a priceless gift
A lesson waiting to be learned

Dearest Mommy,

When you wonder the meaning of life and love
Know that I am with you
Close your eyes and feel me kissing you
In the gentle breeze across your cheek
When you begin to doubt that you shall ever see me again
Quiet your mind and hear me
I am in the whisper of the heavens
Speaking of your love

When you lose your identity
When you question who you are
          Where you are going
Open your heart and see me
I am the twinkle in the stars
          Smiling down upon you
Lighting the path for your journey
When you awaken each morning
Not remembering your dreams
          But feeling content and serene
Know that I was with you
Filling your night with thoughts of me

When you linger in the remnant pain
Wholeness seeming so unfamiliar
Think of me and know that I am with you
Touching you through the shared tears of a gentle friend
Easing the pain

As the sunrise illuminates the desert sky
In that breathtaking glory, awaken your spirit
Think of our time together, all too brief, but ever brilliant
When you were certain of your destiny

Know that God created that moment in time, just for us.

Dearest Mommy, I am with you always.

July 27, 1998

I miss you. Happy Birthday to my special four-year old. Four is such a wonderful age!

The whisper of an angel
Can open Heaven's gate,
A glimpse of faith and courage
A love strong enough to wait,

Whisper you are safe
Whisper softly, angel love,
My heart is aching so
Needing comfort from above,

Tell me you are with me
Whisper gently in my ear,
(You will always be my mommy)
In the quiet I will hear,

My heart still aches to hold you
I close my eyes and see,
Your face now, four years later
And who you were to be,

Though dreams I once held close
In the distance now, so far
Still you're more than just my child
You're the twinkle in the stars,

So I'll hear your angel whispers
"You never need let go,
Hold me, mommy, close within,"
Though the pain and sorrow flow,

One day we shall reunite
Angels whisper words of grace,
And I promise I will hold you
In another time and place.

Happy Birthday, Princess. I miss you!

April 2, 1999

Dear Cheyenne,

I have a new nemesis: the Arizona law that disallows the issuance of birth certificates for children who are born still. I began writing letters to the governor and to legislators. There must be something we can do to change the law and the perception that this policy is acceptable and just.

Some days
Are peaceful
Like still waters
Beauty around each corner
And I wonder, do you walk with me?

But some days still
Are filled with madness
And I cry for you
Search for you
And I wonder
Some days
Do you cry for
and search for
me, too?

Mother's Day 1999

After grieving your death for nearly five years, I have discovered that death is merely a state of being. It does not end love and it cannot end a relationship. So today, my fifth Mother's Day without you, I write down my tearful thoughts.

The love of a mother is immeasurable. A mother's love begins at conception. The wondrous body of a woman nurtures her unborn child. Giving food, nourishment, warmth and shelter. It is an incomprehensible love... she welcomes her newborn with loving arms despite the tremendous physical pain of childbirth... she sacrifices anything to care for her child...her love brings certain death to the enemy, yet a gentle, warm embrace for her child. A mother's love has many faces: A face of peace, kindness, compassion, and tenderness. It is a face of inspiration, light, unconditional love, and undying devotion.

Not even the burning, empty arms of grief can rescind the love of a mother. The love between a mother and her child can never be broken. It is a bond which transcends distance, darkness, and sorrow; a bond which transcends life and death.

Once a mother, always a mother.

September '99

They walked hand in hand down the street
        the sun reflecting shades of shimmering gold in their hair
Their shadows danced, mother and daughter, on this warm September day

I watched from my window
        as the tears swelled my eyes
My palms began to sweat
        and my arms began to ache.

I wondered why there were more children than usual this school year?

I wondered if the mothers would cry
        as their own five-year old waved goodbye-
        for their very first day in kindergarten
But just for one day.

I wondered what it would feel like to be one of them,
        To be part of the Kindergarten Club this year

And I wondered what kindergarten would be like in 1999
Without the little girl, who would have been the star...

December 17, 1999

Dear Cheyenne,

I am writing this at nearly midnight. Lately, I have been very sad. The deaths continue, and I am helpless to stop it. All I can do I cry with the heartbroken families and share their pain. Tonight, I took the kids to a Camp Paz Christmas Party. Camp Paz is the wonderful retreat they attended during the summer for bereaved children. It was at a church quite a distance from our home, but they really wanted to go and revisit the friends they made at camp.

The evening was a wonderful time to reflect. I was an "attendee" this time, instead of my usual "coordinator" role. Thus, I had an opportunity to experience the celebration of remembrance. We sang songs and viewed a slide presentation of camp. During the candle lighting, I broke down, Chey. I was so emotional that I had to leave the auditorium and walk to the back of the room. Tears were pouring down my face, mascara blinding my eyes. Thoughts of, "Why do I keep doing this?" and "I cannot do this anymore, I'm not strong enough," haunted me. I asked for a sign- for strength to continue this work. Your big sister, Stevie Jo, came to the back of the room to check on me.

"Are you okay, Mommy?" she asked. "Yes, Sweetie," I said, "I am just missing your baby sister." Knowing I just needed some time alone, she went back to her seat. With my head down and my heart heavy, I agonized over your death. I wondered why such horrible things happened to such good parents. I struggled because it had been so long since I'd felt your presence close to me. I have been so busy lately that I haven't made time for solitude...to remember you and our experience.

When I lifted my head to wipe my eyes, a miracle occurred. There was a large display shelf with locking glass handing on the back wall of the auditorium. On the shelf was a large wooden sign:

Actual Sign from the night of December 17, 1999

I couldn't believe my eyes! Not just your name, but you are my fourth child too! I began to laugh hysterically. It was, well, such a *literal sign*! So there I was, in all my insanity- laughing, crying- trying to make myself believe what I was seeing with my own eyes!

93

When the ceremony ended, I stood frozen in my place, staring at the sign. I showed everyone who passed the sign; certainly they would never really understand the true significance of it. But still, I had to share it. I asked several people from the church if they knew how the sign got there, or what it was used for, but no one knew. It didn't really matter. I was there at that very moment for a reason. It was a gift. Thank you.

So much has happened since your death, Cheyenne. Your little life, ever so brief, and the lives of so many other children who have died, are touching thousands of people. The pain of never seeing you grow into a beautiful young girl, never seeing your smile, or hearing your voice, or feeling you wraps your arms around my neck...or hearing you call me mommy- that pain is always there. But I hold you in my heart, Cheyenne. Your love and your gifts are far bigger than the pain now.

Though I didn't have enough time to be your mother here on earth, I hope that you realize how much you are loved, and that love I have for you will continue as long as I have breath.

For as long as I live, I am the mother of five children- four who walk and one who soars.

Dear Cheyenne,
It is so hard to imagine that you have been gone so long.

> (Surely, Mommy,
> It seems like yesterday I departed from your loving arms).

Yet still, I search for you in the eyes of children
I yearn to hear your voice in their laughter
I ache to see you
within their shadows that cast playful characters
and daydreams.

> (Oh, Mommy, I have heard your weeping
> And looked upon you with loving eyes,
> during times of cavernous pain
> I have seen your aching body writhe with grief
> I am watchful over you, through your ongoing struggle.
> I would never abandon you).

As I exist in the madness of the world,
My sorrow rooted within the Earth-
I search for the answers I do not expect to find
For I know in my heart
One day, the answers shall find me.

> (Here I await
> My spirit dwells peacefully beyond the silvery stars
> My sorrow, too, rooted deep within the heavens
> Waiting to give substance to your faith
> To answer your whispered calls to me
> To quench the droughts of your questioning).

I love you precious child. Did you know?

> (I know you love me. Don't ever doubt that.
> The veil that lies between us cannot steal your love.
> You gave me life, nurtured within the warmth of your womb).

And time quietly passes,
Remember my child,
that my love for you is stronger than death.

> (I will remember that our love for each other is
> truly stronger than death).

The American Dream

Baseball and apple pie
      White picket fence
            2.5 Children

A good job
Wall Street Success
      A Day at Gymboree

Three weeks paid vacation
To a faraway island
Silver S.U.V.

Braces.

I am not one of them.

My dream is of another world.
I dream of the day
When all babies cry at birth, never silenced by death.

I dream of the day
When every child wakes from his quiescent slumber.

I dream of the day
When every child comes home from prom night.

I dream of the day when every child grows to be old
And all parents die first. As it should be.

I dream of the day
When parents celebrate life, ignorant to any other way.

I dream of the day when others realize how very much it hurts,
and offer unconditional compassion

I dream of the day, when I will hold the little girl whom I buried in 1994.

This is my American Dream.

January 2, 2000

Dear Cheyenne,

As of today, we have sold more than 85,000 Kindness Cards for the project. Its success represents the unification of parents worldwide to remember their child. In hopes for the future, may we continue to share the memory of those loved and lost, so that others may learn, grow, and experience love, compassion, and kindness.

But the miracle of this is not my own. I am not noble. I am not good. This is not about me being an altruist. The choice is not my own. I escape through the only exit that saves me from the debilitating grief. I channel the guilt, sorrow, anger, and sadness through MISS and the Kindness Project - through helping others. It is not by choice. It is what I *must* do.

Governor Hull responded to my letter about the necessary changes to Arizona law in order to provide, not just a death certificate, but also a birth certificate for stillborn infants also. The Registrar of Vital Records called and we are going to meet. I have been in tears of celebration all day.

Come to the stillness
In deafening moments
And I will whisper to you

Come to the light
When the world is dark
And I will show you the way

Come to the warmth
In the chill of grief
And I will wrap my wings of gold
Around you

I will comfort you
With my gifts
Come to the silence
Come to me...

February 17, 2000

I am really angry today. I spent twenty minutes on the phone arguing with the director of a state program that is supposed to monitor laws and protocol regarding child death in Arizona. He is just a very ignorant man who is supposed to be an advocate for children but instead he is worrying about his own agenda. He guaranteed that this idea for birth certificates would never pass in Arizona and told me to give it up. He said I wouldn't even make it to a committee hearing.

I could just scream! I don't understand his objections; it makes no sense at all. Regardless, I won't give up. If I am not heard this year, then I will be back the next year, and the year after that, and the next, and the next. I won't stop until justice prevails.

Anger
Some say it is bad
But it is all in the reputation
Because anger is not bad
It is what you do with the anger that can be bad
Or self-destructive
Or hateful
However,
What you do with anger
Can also be good
And can cause social change
That helps others
And rights the wrongs of the ignorant

September 22, 2000

I taught at the Compassionate Friends Regional Conference on Infant and Toddler Death and its effects. It was a tough class.

I met a man whose 3, 5, and 6 year old children and wife were killed in a house fire. His story was unfathomable. We talked for a long time before and after class. Actually, he talked. There was absolutely nothing I could say or do except cry with him.

I hate it when people say that God never gives you more than you can handle. This is exactly why.

Silence
Is the only thing
I can offer
To show my reverence
Confirmation
for all that you feel
Words are nothing
Meaningless
Only silence
Is sacred enough to offer …
Silence and my tears

March 28, 2001

This was the last day for HB2416, the MISSing Angels bill. The bill states that instead of just issuing a Certificate of Fetal Death for stillborn infants, the state of Arizona would also have to issue a Certificate of Birth resulting in Stillbirth. It would either pass and the law would change or it would be voted out and I'd have to try again next session.

I found a sponsor, Representative Marilyn Jarrett, last year and have been actively educating legislators since then. We made it through the House successfully and the Senate has been very willing to hear the reasoning behind this piece of legislation.

I saw Senator Nichols right before the Health Committee hearing two weeks ago. He gave me a hug and told me that it would pass because "it was right and fair and good for women!" Then, today, just before the final vote he asked me if I remembered what he said (I was pacing back and forth in front of the lobby). I said yes and we hugged again.

I sat in the viewing section of the senate floor with my head buried in David's chest as they read the bill number for final vote. I couldn't bear to look and my body was shaking. David recited the votes as they came in: green, green, green, green, he kept going. With childlike courage, I peeked at the board. As I did, the entire board began to light up with green "ayes" for HB2416. I cannot even describe it. There are no words.

After the unanimous vote, Senator Susan Gerard, Chair of the Health Committee, made a statement that will be engraved in my heart as long as I live:

"The passage of this bill will give much needed respect to those who have experi   enced the stillbirth of a child. It may even be the first step toward increased knowledge about the causes of stillbirth. In addition it makes Arizona the first state in what will hopefully be a national trend toward recognizing the significance of this tr   agedy. I would like to thank Joanne Cacciatore for her leadership and efforts on this bill and her daughter, Cheyenne Cacciatore for whom this act is named."

What more could I say tonight, Cheyenne, except that I have fought for you, and for all the children, and together, we were victorious. I love you. Tonight, I sleep with golden slumbers. Goodnight.

April 19, 2001

Senator Andy Nichols died today. What a terrible, terrible loss for his wife and children, for the Arizona Senate, for the thousands of families and causes he championed for over his lifetime, and for our entire state. And it is a significant loss for me, too. While I did not know him long, the brief time I did know him I felt blessed by his presence. He did so much to help others. It is a very sad, sad day.

I keep remembering his words and reassurances last month and how, during the Health Committee hearing, when he voted on HB2416, he looked over at me as he said "Aye" and smiled in affirmation. I will miss you, Senator Nichols.

I began my volunteer position at the Maricopa County Medical Examiner's Office as a Family Liaison. I call families who have experienced the death of a child or young teenager. I go in one day a week and send follow-up information, advocate for them, provide autopsy report updates, and ensure they are well-connected to the appropriate nonprofit and social service agencies that can help their family get through this difficult time. It is a much-needed service and all the physicians and administrators are so grateful for my presence there. The rewards come, however, when I hang up the phone and a grieving parent says, *"Thank you so much for calling."*

I was left completely alone when you died. No social worker visited. No pastor offered comfort. No doctor sat and cried with me. No one called. No one followed up. I was just left alone. That should never happen, Chey. I vowed to do something about it in 1994. I am making my promise good.

It is easy to get caught up in the chaos of life
And forget
The promises
And commitments
You made while in the abyss
But that is a terrible mistake
For a promise made
At a desperate time
Is one of great importance
Its meaning is more
Than a common promise
It meaning is one of spirit,
Fortitude, and hope
And fulfilling it
Will fulfill you

April 22, 2001

Dear Cheyenne,

I am getting read for the MISS Foundation's first international conference in June.
There is so much going on! We have nearly 100 people already registered and are
expecting nearly 200 by the time June arrives.

Anyway, through a bizarre twist of fate, I ended up meeting Ken Ross, the son of Dr.
Elisabeth Kubler-Ross! After learning all that I had done with the MISS Foundation,
he gave me Dr. Ross' number and told me to call her. He said she'd want to meet me
in person. So I did. I am going to visit her next week! I can hardly wait! She has been
my hero since I read her first book (the one that saved me) right after you died.

We are going to give Dr. Ross the Platinum Wings Lifetime Achievement Award at
the June conference, so Randy and I are working on a slide presentation to honor her
life's work!

I went to the cemetery today. It was beautiful outside. I saw Mathilda there and
gave her a rose for Victor. She told me that life is a bit easier now but that she still
misses him very much. I told her that missing our loved ones is what we do best
around here...

The sun sets
And she rises
But in between
Life is full of change
Every day something new and different
Grief sets
Grief rises
Some things, however, never change

July 27, 2001

Dear Cheyenne,

I can recall, with unmitigated detail, July 27, 1994. The smell of the room, the silence of your birth, the incessant ache in my body, the fading of my cognitions from terror to disbelief to numbness. I can remember what it felt like...holding your lifeless body in my arms, pleading with you to breathe. I can remember the whispers outside my door and the triumphant protests of the other babies emerging from their mothers' wombs. When I quiet my mind, it is all so clear.

Seven years seems so long ago. I have lived twenty lives since your death. I have watched other children die. I have not only lived it but I have watched the metamorphosis from despair and horror to peace and acceptance in the other families. There is some comfort to helping others, Chey. But how I wish you were here- When I awoke this morning, I awoke to thoughts of sneaking into your bedroom, across the hall, presumably pink with mermaids and beating hearts, waking you up by jumping on your bed and smothering you with seven kisses, one for each year. Singing happy birthday in my best off-key voice. Things would be so different. Oh, God, Cheyenne, I love you! I miss you...

What kinds of things
Does a seven-year old do?
Does she try braids
And challenge authority?
Does she cry at night
And jump on her bed?
Does she steal her brother's toys
And play with make-up
And brush her mother's hair?
Or
Does she brush her wings
And sing with the choir?
Does she play with angels
and jump on clouds?
Does she send her messages
And affirm her presence?
And does she touch
the Face of God?

August 2, 2001

Dear Cheyenne,

With the simple words *"We all know this change should have happened a long time ago,"* Arizona Governor Jane D. Hull picked up her pen and signed "The MISSing Angels" bill, HB 2416, into law. It takes effect August 9, 2001.

After more than a year of lobbying, meeting personally and telling your story over and over again, I still cannot believe the bill passed, Cheyenne. This is truly amazing! No other state in the U.S. issues birth certificates for stillborns - Arizona will be the first.

I am in tears. Overwhelmed. From this day forward, no parent of a baby who dies during delivery will have to fight for a birth certificate. Finally, one small step toward justice has been won. I love you! I can barely believe it! This has been one of the greatest accomplishments of my life.

Bill Signing with Governor Hull

Love weeps
In the hallway near the bookcase
Across from the room
That would have been hers
For seven years now

Love weeps
In the abandonment
Of the night, where no one can see, or hear
(They cannot fix it anyway)

Sorrow is love's pulse
And the only path
Leading to the escape from the maze
So love *must* weep

It wasn't my choice
To experience this love
So profound
That it would personify itself
Into loyal tears who would visit daily
And Herculean sadness that would steal my own breath
As I beg impunity

I would rather have the love that laughs and runs
In the sunshine
And rides off on the horse into the sunset
And ignorantly defies the truth

That love weeps.

August 19, 2001

Monsoon season is here again. Unpredictable just like grief...

The rain fell
From the inside
Of the store, I saw
Monsoons intruding upon summer
Delivering fury from the heavens
Onto the asphalt

I hesitated
Should I wait out the storm?
But she has taught me
Not to wait
And what is wrong
With wet hair and sticky clothes?

And so, with intentions
Of running through the lot, safely to the car
Leaving behind the croissants and paper towels
The door opened automatically
But the plan was interrupted

She caught my eye, to the left
A mother and her little girl
She was protecting her
From the rain
She removed her coat, kindergarten-yellow
Held it over her daughter's head
She was afraid of wet hair and sticky clothes
Maybe pneumonia?
And they ran
Through the puddles, and they splashed, and they laughed.
And then safely got into their car.

My mind attacked me as I stood frozen on the sidewalk
I wasn't expecting the assault
Delivering fury from the Heavens
It caught me off guard and
The video rewound to August of 1994

The monsoons that fell, suddenly
Like your death
(Sorrow that intruded upon the joy of delivery)

I was watching the television
But it wasn't on
(As frequently my mind)

I rushed to the window.
Rain began to pour
Like the tears, since your death
Panic struck like lightning
And as any good mother
Needing to protect her little girl
From wet hair, sticky clothes, and maybe pneumonia,
Systematically, taking what I would need
To shelter her from the storm
Primary blue tarp (as an umbrella)
And a mother's heart for comfort...
But then, the shovel hidden beneath the gardening tools
Collecting dust, as her nursery
Screamed, "Take me! Save your little girl!"

I could not rescue her from the storm that day
As I tried to leave, her father pulled me from my car
Kicking and fighting, I protested, pleaded
But he would not allow me to go (I hated him)
To protect my child
As any good mother should

Her body, surely drenched
No splashing, no laughing
And through the night
Thoughts of wet hair, sticky clothes, and pneumonia
Haunted and scorned me
Sleep does not come easy
For a mother who cannot safeguard her child

We did not get into our car, safely
I could not deliver her from death.

September 11, 2001

Dear Cheyenne,

Something very horrible happened this morning. Four planes crashed, two into the World Trade Center, one in Pennsylvania, and one into the Pentagon. So many, many people died. It was like a nightmare. I cannot even write today. I am in shock. Grief images plaster every television station. The horror of this event is surreal. Surely, there are thousands dead.

You cannot isolate grief
When one person dies, it affects the community
In a profound way
Each person's life
Is tremendously valuable
And is linked to every other person
We are all a part
Of the cycle of life
Of Mother Earth
And Father Time
Of each other
Each death
Is a loss to us all...
Every death
Affects each of us
In some small, or maybe not-so-small, way

September 26, 2001

Dear Cheyenne,

Elisabeth and I watched a special on Dr. Martin Luther King, Jr. The documentary focused on his movement against hate and prejudice, ignorance and violence. There is still so much of that prevalent in our society, even decades after his death. Yet, the events of September 11th have continued to affect every person in this country and around the world in a very profound way. Elisabeth and I agreed that this is a historical moment of epiphanies; people are experiencing a collective grief that no one has ever witnessed. Even the media has expanded their discussions on the emotional aspects of death and its effects on a family and the community at large.

Still, it seems strange to me. Every day, thousands and thousands of adults and children die. And while the manner in which September 11th occurred was senseless and devastating, people die every day in senseless and devastating ways and they are too soon forgotten or overlooked by the public and media: abducted and murdered children, women raped and killed, disease, car accidents, fires, malnourished children, and the list goes on. I am hopeful that this public forum we now have will serve to open the eyes of our culture- death surrounds us. Every person needs the degree of community intervention, support, and compassion that is being offered to the grieving family members of the September 11th victims. Maybe it is through this lesson, we will all truly learn.

"The most beautiful people we have known are those who have known defeat,
known suffering, known struggle, known loss, and have found their way out of the depth
These persons have an appreciation, a sensitivity
and an understanding of life that fills them with compassion,
gentleness, and a deep loving concern.
Beautiful people do not just happen."
- Elisabeth Kubler-Ross

October 4, 2001

Awesome news! Utah, Massachusetts, and Indiana have all filed the MISSing Angels bill in their legislature! This means they are moving toward issuing birth certificates for all children who die prior to their birth. To me, this represents the second monumental step on behalf of these families!

The kids are doing great. We still talk about you all the time. In fact, Joshua was in school and they asked him to draw a picture of his family. When he did, he included you. They questioned him about it and he said that he has a sister who went to Heaven before he was born (I promised you that he'd know all about you!).

I see Elisabeth at least once a week. We go shopping, out to eat, or just eat popcorn and watch movies (we watched "Chocolat" last weekend and she loved it)! I have learned so much about her. She calls herself a Swiss hillbilly, she hates 'phony-baloneys,' she loves chocolate and E.T. and she is a wonderful friend. I love and cherish my time with her and told her she's not allowed to "take-off" until we have more time together (she even helps me with homework)!

We have our fundraiser BBQ in a few weeks. I am going to invite Nana and Papa and the rest of the family. Even though they haven't really been involved in what the MISS Foundation does, I am hoping this event will be something they'd participate in. I wish they would remember you and miss you like I do.

A pause in life is good
Pause to say "I love you"
Pause to say "I am so sorry"
Pause to say "I am here for you"
Just pause
And remember

October 27, 2001

Dear Cheyenne,

Today was the Glendale Active 20-30 Club's BBQ to benefit the MISS Foundation. It was a lot of fun! So many families attended! We raised more than $1500.00 for our Family Services Programs. Many companies donated items that we could auction and there were even horseback rides for children.

The best part was that our entire family came. Nana, for the first time *ever*, made a donation in your memory! On the way home, I started to cry. It meant a lot to me. She said, "This is for Cheyenne." I am very grateful.

We now have eight MISS chapters in Arizona and new chapters are forming all around the world! We have them in California, Washington D.C., New York, Texas, Ohio, Mexico City - well, all over! This is a clear demonstration of the need for our organization! Last week we sent thousands of children's grief support packets and books to the families who survived 9-11. We had seven volunteers at our house putting them together to ship out. United Parcel Service is shipping the boxes for free. The website now receives more than 1,000 hits a day and I get about 200-250 emails from grieving families everyday. We've sold more than 330,000 Kindness Project cards. We have accomplished the very thing we set out to do: No one has to be alone anymore when their child dies and professionals are starting to understand how significant this loss is for families. It is like a caring community of compassion. A miracle.

> *"Never doubt that a small group of committed citizens can change the world. indeed, it's the only thing that ever has."*
> Margaret Mead

November 4, 2001

Dear Cheyenne,

Today, your grandmother joined you. My mother, the woman who gave me life, died. I feel so many different things that I am unable to articulate into words. My mother is dead. I was with her when she died after they disconnected her from life support. All the children were there, despite some peripheral concerns, and they handled it quite well, even Joshua, who, at almost five, is mature beyond his years.

I called Elisabeth and cried my eyes out. She didn't say much except the perfect things to say- that she loved me, that I *should* feel sad, that she is sorry.

It is now nearly midnight. Sleep eludes me yet again. I seem to be numb, an all-too familiar feeling of seven years ago. Cheyenne, death is so hard.

Take care of NaNa. Show her around. And ask her all about your mother and the mischief I caused when I was little. I am certain she'll have fun telling you *all* about your mother.

I can barely believe that I have buried my little girl and now I have to bury my mother. The two most important women figures in my life are gone.

I've always known
It would happen one day
That Death would visit
And Grief would become my constant companion, again
I suppose
This is the price
I must pay
For love

Love is worth it all...

November 9, 2001

Dear Cheyenne,

On November 5, the day after Nana died, I decided that to honor her, I would put together a video collection of photos of her life. I wanted to set it to music and play it at the funeral today.

I spent four days sifting through old photographs, crying, laughing, and reminiscing. I managed to assemble a chronological perspective of her life in a constellation of images, from her infancy through her marriage, the births of all four of her children, and all her grandchildren. But then came the dilemma. I had plenty of pictures of Nana with your three brothers and sister, but I had none with you. Oh Chey, how I cried and cried. I wanted them all to know that indeed, she had another grandchild, one who died too soon. But I had no way to put you in the video. Then I remembered what she had given me the day you died. It was a little plaque that I have hanging on my wall that was engraved with the saying, "A mother holds her child hand awhile, her heart forever ...In memory of Cheyenne, 7-27-94, Love Nana and Papa."

Perfect, I thought! I'd put this into the video! But I was so disappointed today when I picked up the videos for the funeral. The video producer said that it would not photo well and that he couldn't include it in the final version. I felt tremendously guilty. You were nowhere to be found in her final services and I couldn't do anything about it.

After the graveside service, we went back to Nana and Papa's house for that antiquated ritual of post-funeral smorgasbord (I have never liked or understood that? The last thing I want to do is eat when I feel so bad inside?). I ran into Linda there. I haven't seen her in eight years or so. She came up and gave me a hug and said how sorry she was. Then she handed me a Hallmark bag and said she'd stopped by the store to pick up a sympathy card for me but that instead, she walked over to a shelf and picked up a small frame and knew she "had to buy it" for me. She said she didn't know why, but that she was compelled. I opened it. The saying inside the frame said, "A mother holds her child hand awhile, her heart forever."

I went into the bathroom and I cried.

And I cried.

Self Help Articles and Resources

If your child has just died: Your options and choices

- Take pictures. Hold your child. Take time to say goodbye. Do not feel intimidated or pressured by what others may think. Quiet your mind and listen to your heart. If you are unsure whether you want photos, take them anyway. You do not have to develop the film until you are ready, if ever.

- Videotape the service.

- Save everything! Clip a lock of hair, the wristband from the hospital and any other item of memoriam that can be included in a special place with your child's other belongings.

- If your child dies at birth or shortly after, it is okay to open your child's eyes.

- Try to be an integral part of planning your child's funeral and memorial service. While it is very difficult, by participating in the plans, you will ensure that the choices you make for the services will be the right ones for your family.

- You have the option to dress and bathe your child.

- Tell people if they have said something that hurts you. The only way that people will learn sensitivity is through gentle education.

- Invite family, including siblings, into the room to say goodbye. Children need to be included in family ritual.

- Participate in the Kindness Project (see www.missfoundation.org). Some families ask for donations to a nonprofit group, like the MISS Foundation or other philanthropy movement, in lieu of flowers to honor a child who has died. Others ask for a stuffed animal which they can then donate to a police or fire department for other children.

- Find a place to go to meditate. Alone time is often helpful.

- Talk about your child anytime you want to.

- Attend a support group in your area at least three times. Support groups are a great way to meet people who feel the same way and understand your grief. The first few meetings may seem uncomfortable, but give it at least three tries before you give up. A support group community will also afford you an opportunity to reach out and help someone else who may be earlier in his or her grief.

- Keep a daily journal.

- If you are married or have a significant other, try not to shut them out. Remember that women and men express grief differently. Try not to judge one another or assume you know what they are feeling. Focus on open but nonjudgmental communication.

- Get immediate, and if necessary, ongoing support for your surviving children to assess their coping skills and how the death has affected them. Often, parents are so consumed with their own grief experience, that children, sometimes unable to articulate their need for help into words, are forgotten.

- Do not feel that you must take your child's room apart or take the nursery down immediately. You can do this in your own time. If you do pack your child's things away, do not give away all their belongings. Save the meaningful items that hold a special place in your heart.

- Seek counseling if the grief becomes too much to bear.

Grief plays funny tricks on the mind. You may find yourself being forgetful, losing things, sleeping a great deal or not wanting to go outside your home. It is all part of the journey. There is a light; however, we all arrive at different points during the process.

Immediate family members, including grieving children, should be involved in planning the funeral and memorial services. Those who did not participate often say they felt uncomfortable with the choices others made for their child's services. Well meaning relatives and friends may try to assume the burden to save the parents from the pain. While the process will certainly be difficult, it is also a critical step in the healing process.

Selecting the Funeral Home

Base your selection on several factors. Call or visit funeral homes that you are interested in. Be sure to tell the funeral director that you have just experienced the death of a child family member. Their attitude should be sensitive and gentle. Ensuring that the professionals involved in planning the services are sensitive to your needs as a bereaved parent is important.

If you are comfortable with the director's level of awareness and sensitivity, you can schedule an appointment to review services options. Consider all the options that they have available to you carefully; issues including location, flexibility of service options, coordination with clergy and the cemetery you have chosen, and payment arrangements. Be sure to make any special desires known so the funeral home is able to prepare and coordinate the arrangements according to your wishes. If the event becomes too difficult for you at any point, ask a family member or support group volunteer to convey your requests for the memorial service.

Traditional Funeral

There are two types of funerals. One is with your child's body present so that family members and friends may have the opportunity to say goodbye. This ritual is called a viewing. The other is without your child's body present. You may choose an open or closed casket memorial service. If you choose to have your child's body present, consider decorating his or her casket with pictures of the family, stuffed animals, toys, flowers, and other memorial items. A common myth surrounding burial is that all bodies must be embalmed. States laws may vary on this, however, in some cases, this is a personal decision. Express your questions and concerns to the director.

Cremation

If you are considering cremation, think about what you would like to do with your child's ashes before making your final decision. If you cremate, you may keep the ashes in an urn at your home, you may bury the ashes (interred) with a memorial headstone, or you may scatter the ashes at a special location. If you choose to scatter the ashes, we strongly recommend that you keep a portion of the ashes. There are special boxes, charm necklaces, and mini urns that are available to keep a small portion of the ashes in. If you decide to cremate, you should still have a memorial service for family and friends.

If you are feeling pressured into cremation either by a lack of funds, time, or confusion, ask a professional to assist you in exploring all your options and the long term consequences of each possible choice in order to minimize the potential for regrets.

For some parents, having a special place to go and care for their child's body is cathartic. An occasional visit to the cemetery where your child is buried or the ashes are interred can have a special healing effect. This can be a place to go on your child's birthday or other holiday. Furthermore, on days when grief is particularly difficult, a cemetery can be a serene place to remember your child and gather your thoughts.

Memorial Services

It is important to have a memorial service for the benefit of surviving family members. Memorial services can be held in various locations such as the funeral home, graveside at the cemetery, in a church, in a special garden, or even at your home. If you have made the decision to scatter your child's ashes in a special location, you may have a memorial service, called a committal service, at that location.

Include children of all ages in the memorial service if they are willing to participate. Offer them an opportunity to speak, read a letter or a poem to their brother or sister, and even help make decisions. Encourage siblings to draw a picture or write a letter and allow them to place it in the casket with their sibling. Choosing a special toy or memorial item from home is helpful. Older siblings may want to help carry the casket at the cemetery. Including siblings in the service will bring them realization of the death of the baby, and give them special memories they will carry their lifetime.

Your minister, a staff member of the funeral home, or even a friend or family member can direct the service. We recommend that you videotape the service. It may be painful to look at the video immediately after the death of your child; however, someday you may want to have it available to you. Consider songs that you would like to be played, poetry read in memory of your child, and having your child baptized if you are spiritual and had not done so in the hospital.

Ideas for a Special Goodbye:

-Choose a special song to eulogize your child. Listen to the words for meaning. Print the words to the song on special paper for the memorial service.

-Bring a special stuffed animal such as a lamb, toys from siblings, cards and letters from siblings, a special necklace for your child to be buried with.

-Choose a special outfit (perhaps the siblings could assist in choosing the outfit) and a special blanket. Don't forget booties and perhaps a bonnet or headband (for a girl). Be sure they have removed your child's identification bracelet prior to burial for keepsake.

-The mother and father should try to write a letter to their child. A close friend or family member can read the letter on behalf of the parents. The letter should be about the feelings of grief, loss and love for the child.

-Open casket services help to make an infant more "real" to others.

-Spend time holding and rocking your child prior to the service. You can take the baby out of the casket and hold him or her.

-Ask others to send stuffed animals or toys in lieu of flowers. After the services, you can donate to a local charity on behalf of your child.

-Make a tape of your own favorite songs so you are not limited to the choice of the funeral home.

-Close the casket for the final time.

-The family can request to shovel the first dirt.

-A balloon release is a warm tribute to the significance of the child's life.

-A ceremony at sundown is beautiful. Consider a graveside unity candlelight service. This is a service where one larger candle is lit, and each person lights his or her candle off the main unity candle in honor of the child.

-If you do not want to have a post-funeral reception, don't. This is a ritual that some like and others strongly dislike. Do what is best for you and your family.

Our last goodbye
Should be as beautiful
Special
And perfect
As you are to me.
Our last goodbye
Will remain inscribed upon my heart
Until the day I die

FUNERAL/MEMORIAL PREPARATION WORKSHEET

❖ Name of funeral home/mortuary:_____

    Name of funeral director:_____

    Address:_____

    Phone:_____

❖ Date and Time of service: _____

❖ Location of service: _____

❖ Clergy/Person presiding over ceremony:_____

                        Phone:_____

❖ Additional person(s)/children participating in ceremony:
(pallbearers, writing letter, drawing pictures, balloon/butterfly release, oversee guest registry book, etc...)

    Name:_____ Duty:_____

         _____   _____

         _____   _____

         _____   _____

❖ Reading of parents/siblings letters written to child(if applicable):

    Mother's letter to be read by:_____

    Father's letter to be read by: _____

    Sibling's letter to be read by:_____

❖ Music selections:

    Song:_____ Artist:_____

        _____   _____

        _____   _____

        _____   _____

❖ Poetry/Scripture selections:

_____ Read by:_____

_____   _____

_____   _____

_____   _____

❖ Things to include in ceremony program/eulogy: (picture of child and/or family, words of song or poem, hand/footprints, special message about child)

_____

_____

_____

❖ Items to be placed in casket (if applicable):_____

_____

_____

_____

❖ Items to be displayed at service:_____

_____

_____

❖ Memorial contributions (in lieu of flowers):_____

_____

❖ Florist choice (if applicable):_____

                    Phone:_____

❖ Additional contacts:_____ Phone:_____

Music Therapy....Meaningful Memorial Songs

Artist Randy Thompson (Inspirational)
Song "A Mother's Love" Title "In Remembrance"

Artist Vineyard Music Group (Inspirational)
Song "Eternity" Title "Light the Fire Again" 1 800-852-VINE

Artist Patty Loveless (Western)
Song "How Can I Help You Say Goodbye"

Artist Eric Clapton (Easy Rock)
Song "Tears in Heaven"

Artist Celine Dion (Contemporary)
Song "Fly" & "My Heart Goes On (Theme from the Titanic)"

Donna Lewis
Song "Silent World "

Artist Kenny Loggins (Pop)
Song " Somewhere Out There"

Artist Richard Marx (Contemporary)
Song "An Angel's Lullaby"

Artist Garth Brooks (Country)
Song "The Dance"

Artist Mariah Carey (Pop)
Song "Butterfly"

Artist Amy Grant (Christian)
Song "Somewhere Down the Road"

Artist LeeAnn Rimes (Country) or various artists
Song "Amazing Grace"

The Choir (Artistic Modern rock, Christian)
Song "Sad Face" Album Title "Chase the Kangaroo"

Artist Colin Raye (Country)
Song "Love Remains"

Artist Vince Gill (Country)
Song "Go Rest High on the Mountain"

Other Ritual

Dr Sukie Miller describes ritual as the "antidote to powerlessness." Here are some ideas for ongoing ritual activities that may help bring healing after a child's death:

Memorial Album-Create a memorial album for your son or daughter. Include a locket of hair, identification bracelets, birth cards and anything else you desire. If you have other children, allow them to write their feelings and thoughts.

Charitable Donations- Offer a memorial donation on behalf of your child. Many philanthropic groups will send special thank you cards to commemorate your child's life. Be sure to include this in your child's memorial album.

Framing Pictures- Purchase special frames for your child's photographs and hang the pictures in your home, especially if your child did not live long. You may choose a particular wall where many family pictures are displayed.

Memorial Locket- There are many beautiful lockets that you can purchase which allow you to display a picture of your child. Have the locket engraved with a special message or saying.

Birthstone Rings & Necklaces- Rings, necklaces or bracelets with your child's birthstone often have gender sensitive shaped children.

Memory Box- Keep a memory box with your child's items. Such items might include a blanket from the hospital, booties, your baby album, stuffed animals, medical records from their birth, sympathy cards from friends and family, and any other memorial items you may have.

Plant a Memorial Tree- Some states will allow you to participate in a tree-planting program at a local park in memory of your child. If that is not an option, consider a tree in your yard, or at your church with a plaque dedicating the tree to your child. You can expand it into a memorial or contemplation garden which includes engraved bricks, flowers, and angel statues.

The Kindness Project- Participate in random acts of kindness! This is a wonderful movement that has brought significant healing in communities! For more information, visit our website at www.missfoundation.org.

Am I Losing My Mind?

In working with the bereaved, one of the most prevalent concerns is questioning feelings, emotions and reaction to grief. I frequently hear, "Am I crazy?" Certainly the vast array of overwhelming emotions can surprise those in early grief. It can be frightening, intimidating, and confusing. However, one of the primary reasons support groups are so effective in helping bereaved parents work their way through grief is the confirmation they lend when others share similar feelings and thoughts. There seems to be an intimate connection which occurs when the newly bereaved person discovers his or her "irrational thoughts" are not abnormal for others experiencing the same grief.

Here are some physical and emotional symptoms not uncommon for those in grief:

- A feeling of tightness in the throat or heaviness in the chest with rapid breathing. You may feel as if you are experiencing a panic attack and have no control over where or when this occurs.
- An empty feeling in their stomach and loss (or gain) of appetite. Call your physician if this continues longer than several weeks
- Pain and/or nausea in stomach. Once again, call your physician if this persists
- Restlessness and a desire for activity, but have difficulty concentrating. Focusing is difficult and forgetfulness quite apparent
- Being in a trance-like state, sitting for hours and staring
- The feeling as though your child's death didn't actually happen; (this may include trying to find your child or repeatedly checking his room or crib)
- Dizziness/disorientation
- Other somatic manifestations
- Loss of appetite
- Weight gain
- Intentional isolation from family and friends
- Feeling as if life has no meaning
- Negotiating in your mind for your child's safe return
- Replaying the details of the events surrounding your child's death and even changing the outcome
- Sudden interest in death and/or the after life
- Frequent, often public, panic attacks
- Sensing your child's presence. For many, this is quite comforting
- Frequent headaches
- Impatience with the tedious day to day chores around the house
- Ambivalence toward surviving children. This can be surprising for many. However, keep in mind that grief is hard work and takes a lot of energy. So much energy, in fact that a parent may not be prepared to expend equal amounts of energy disciplining or caring for surviving children immediately after the death. It may be helpful to ask family members for help so that you can spend some time alone and take care of yourself during the first few months.
- Difficulty sleeping or falling asleep too easily. Even having recurring dreams or visions of your loved one

- Sleeping all day or feeling like you do not want to get out of bed and face the world
- Feeling debilitating guilt or angry. These two emotions are particularly difficult to overcome in the grief process. Many parents find themselves plagued with the "would've, should've, could've" thoughts.

Just knowing that all these feelings and emotions are a normal part of the grief journey helps many parents. No, you are not crazy at all. Perhaps, a little irrational behavior or affect is justifiable in the case of a child's has death. There is no rationalizing or understanding for families going through this difficult life experience. Acknowledging and working through these feelings won't magically dissipate these emotions suddenly one morning. But gradually, healing comes. Through the love for your child, healing will come.

Support Groups & Resources

M.I.S.S. Foundation
National Chapter Locator
Call or email us to find a chapter in your area
P.O. Box 5333
Peoria, Arizona 85385
URL: www.missfoundation.org or our former location www.misschildren.org
623-979-1000 Fax 623-979-1001

Program Directors:
Founder: Joanne Cacciatore-Garard   email Joanne@missfoundation.org
Toddler Death: Katie Hodge   email Katie@missfoundation.org
Fatal Birth Anomalies: Angela Iverson   email Angela@missfoundation.org
Grieving Fathers: Gregg Carder   email Gregg@missfoundation.org
Special Events Chair: Tammy Haimovitz   email Tammy@missfoundation.org

Compassionate Friends (International)
National Chapter 1-630-990-0010
URL: www.compassionatefriends.org

National Stillbirth Society (NSS)
President Richard Olsen
602 216 6600

Anencephaly Research Helpline
(800) 588-6464

National Share Office
St Joseph Health Center
300 First Capitol Dr
St Charles, Mo 63301
(314) 947-6164

Hygeia Foundation
www.hygeia.org
Dr. Michael Berman, Founder

Centering Corporation
1531 N Saddle Creek Road
Omaha, Ne 68104
(402) 553-1200

Center for Loss in Multiple Birth
P.O. Box 1064
Palmer, Ak 99645
(907) 746-6123

Pregnancy and Infant Loss Center
1421 E Wayzata Blvd
Wayzata, Mn 55391
(612) 473-9372

RTS Bereavement Services
1910 South Avenue
La Crosse, Wi 54601
(608) 791-4747

SIDS Alliance
National Chapter 1-800-221-SIDS
URL: www.sidsalliance.org

Sidelines for high-risk pregnancies
National Chapter 1-714-497-2265
URL: www.sidelines.org

AGAST – Grandparent Grief Support Group
National Chapter 1-888-774-7437

Red Means Stop Coalition
Reducing intersection collision deaths
602.323.9163
www.redmeansstop.org

Common Myths about the Death of Your Child

Myth: The younger the child, the less intense your pain should be.
Truth: Even though society may grant less validity to grieve for infants and stillborn babies, the truth is that the love of a parent is not contingent upon the amount of time we had with our child. Love simply cannot be measured in time. Some may try to "prorate" grief. If a ten-year-old dies, it is worth "*x*" amount of pain... if a one year old dies, it is worth "*y*" amount of pain ... if a one day old dies, that is worth only "*z*" amount of pain. Would it be easier to bury a child today or would it be easier to bury them one year from now? It is an impossible question to answer. There is no easier time, no lesser pain. It is horrible whenever it happens.

Myth: It has been six months, you should be over this by now.
Truth: You will never "be over" the pain. This is not a transitory experience, but rather, each day may bring new awareness of loss and thus resultant grief. When a child dies, the family will grieve their entire lifetime for the child they *should* have with them. When others think the family should have *gotten over it by now,* they are confusing the significant impact of the death of a child with an event of much lesser significance. A person can get over the loss of a job, a broken bone, a lost job, or a friendship gone awry. The death of a child, at any age and from any circumstance , is a life changing and tragic event that can never be forgotten. Most people, however, eventually learn the skills necessary to cope with the pain. Day to day life will never be "normal" and may never feel the same again, but time does help to ease the pain and eventually, recognize the many gifts of the child who died.

Myth: Sleeping pills, drugs, antidepressants, or alcohol are the only answer
Truth: Psychoanalyst, Sigmund Freud, discusses the three responses of human beings who have suffered the loss of their 'love object.' He says that people use 1) powerful deflection 2) substitutive satisfaction and 3) intoxication. While these choices may not be the healthiest, they certainly may seem to be the easiest responses, at least, in the short-term. However, some parents who use drugs or use alcohol after the death of their child feel that they may have postponed the inevitable. Grief is hard work, demanding, physically exhausting, and mentally draining. Using the analogy of a financial loan we observe how important it is, however, to deal with the feelings of grief. When a person takes a loan out with a bank, they are aware that they must eventually pay back the loan. The longer the person waits to repay the money, the higher the interest rates and penalties. Indescribable feelings of grief are a **normal** reaction to one of the most difficult experiences of a human being. Only a therapist working with a physician is qualified to assess for the need for long-term anti-depressant use.

Myth: Another child is the answer to the grief.
Truth: Your child's life is worth all the pain you feel. While another child will fill your empty, aching arms, it will never replace your child who died. Allow yourself time to grieve for your child. Do not rush yourself. Another child may complicate and delay the grief process for you, your surviving children, your spouse, and the new child. Be careful not to venture into an unprepared pregnancy too soon after the death of your beloved child.

Myth: You need to forget your child and go on with your life.

Truth: Some people admonish parents for keeping photographs of your deceased child in your home, if you still attend support group meetings, or if you memorialize your child years after his or her death. Your faithfulness to your child's memory is to be commended! Do not let others discourage your gift of dedication. Marcel Proust says, "Unless we remember, we cannot understand."

Myth: You will soon become yourself again.

Truth: The former 'you' probably experienced a metaphorical death when your child died. You may recognize remnant pieces of the former self remaining, however, you are unlikely to ever feel like the exact person you were before your child's death. Be patient with your new self. Your child's death has changed many things about you and you will need time to reacquaint yourself with the new person you have become!

Myth: Support groups are for weak people.

Truth: The death of a child is the most isolating and lonely event in a human's life. Many grieving parents say that friends become strangers and strangers become friends. How can any one truly understand the depth of this pain if they have never experienced it? For example, a woman who has struggled with obesity all her life who finally made a decision to lose weight and become healthy again will need special care. Courageously, she checks herself into a weight loss clinic. But the mentor assigned to help her through her struggle wears a size three in ladies clothing and has never been overweight a day in her life. How can the mentor understand the pain, struggles, and fears? Support groups, like the ones held through the MISS Foundation, are facilitated by parents who have personally experienced this tragedy. They are a safe haven for parents to share their pain with others who have faced many of the same feelings. Many support group members are courageous and compassionate people who have dedicated their lives to helping newly bereaved parents find hope and peace in their life.

Myth: I am going crazy.

Truth: Every parent who has gone through the death of a child feels they are crazy at some point. The vast array of emotions is overwhelming. Many experience emotions we never knew we could feel. The usual routine of day-to-day life suddenly annoys us. We feel out of place even amongst the closest of family and friends. We cannot attend baby showers or birthday parties. We may feel too weak and drained to get out of bed in the morning. Once enjoyed activities become dreaded tasks. Some are unable to perform and focus at work, while others may become completely absorbed in their career attempting to escape the pain. Some express that the grief has become unbearable; they prayed God would take them. Grief is a roller coaster ride. Some days we find laughter and joy. Other days there is a black cloud lingering over us. Who wouldn't feel crazy undergoing all these emotions?

Even though it may feel like it, you aren't crazy. You are a grieving parent, simply missing what should have been in your life. Be patient and kind to yourself. The longing for your child will never disappear, however, time grants us moments of peace in between the tidal waves of pain. Allow those moments to bring you closer to your child's love and the gifts they have left for you to discover.

The Unedited Truth about Grief
Quotes from parents who have walked the journey

"I was always really angry, even to this day. No one can do anything to take the pain away and that is the hardest to accept. So they would end up saying the wrong thing. I'd feel like screaming. Just let me be- my child has died. Just let me be- let me be angry."
Arleen Sheppard, Mother of Scotti Denise Sheppard *, born January 4, 1991*
Died July 22, 1992 of drowning while in the care of the babysitter

"My son's death crushed me completely. The weight is more than I can bear. They say that some day I'll be happy again. The wait is more than I can bear. I spoke those words on May 15, 1993, four months after my son's death. (Now nearly five years later,) I am happy again, despite the fact that the pain is still there and always will be. "
Ruth Gregory, Mother of Timothy Joseph Jones *, born June 12, 1976*
Died January 7, 1993 in an automobile accident

"My son has helped make me who I am today and I am forever grateful for his existence. He has taught me so much about life yet he never spoke a word."
Dean Synan, Father of Justin Synan *, born October 4, 1982*
Died January 25, 1983, Viral Meningitis

"People think you're not handling it because you're crying. Crying is handling it. It is a normal part of the process."
Linda Schill, Mother of David Lawrence Baker *, born September 11, 1981*
Born still after an automobile accident

"I really regret not holding Caitlin. She is my child- a part of me. I needed to bond with her and never got that chance. Whatever you do, hold your child. It is a deep regret that I will live with the rest of my life."
Julie White, Mother of Caitlin Marie White *, born February 25, 1995*
Born still due to unknown cause at 38 weeks gestation

"You will not ever forget your child. It has been nearly forty years since our son died. We have never forgotten him"
Mary Gagliano, Mother of Salvatore Gagliano, Jr I *, born April 1958*
Died April 1958, suspected hypoxia due to prolonged labor

"My strongest belief is that you should grieve as long as you need to and however you see fit. Sometimes people think you're crying too much but don't listen to them. Don't be afraid to show your emotions. Talking, yelling, crying and laughter were all a very big part of my grief."
Esther Grant, Mother of Cara Alyssa Grant *, Born February 2, 1994*
Died February 4, 1994, Hypoplastic Left Heart Syndrome

"I held my baby but only for a few minutes. I didn't hold her long enough. I didn't really look at her or unwrap the blanket. In retrospect, I wish I would have spent more time holding her, looking at her feet and hands and making memories with her."
Jodi Lackey, Mother of Samantha Lackey , born January 4, 1997
Born still at 20 weeks gestation to a placenta accident

"Every anniversary date that goes by is not any different than any other day of the year without our child. It is just another day that our child is not with us. You miss them just as much any other day. Remember that."
Tracey Montgomery, Mother of Emma Grace Montgomery , born December 11, 1996
Died January 15, 1997, Mitochondrial Depletion Disorder

"I never imagined anyone else could feel the kind of grief that I am feeling."
Joy Moore, Mother of Annie and G racie Moore , born November 1, 1997
Born still at 35 weeks gestation

"Above all else, be supportive of your spouse, and look to your spouse for support. Let love, friendship and time bring comfort."
Tom Johnson, Father of Hunter Michael Johnson , born April 28, 1997
Died April 28, 1997, born premature at 23 weeks gestation

"Don't let anyone belittle or minimize the pain that you are feeling. It doesn't matter when your child died; in utero, two days, two months, or twenty years. You still lost a part of your present and future. Because of that, you will never be the same."
Traci Johnson, Mother of Hunter Michael Johnson , born April 28, 1997
Died April 28, 1997, born premature at 23 weeks gestation

"The one thing I would have done differently is to hold Austin at the funeral home. No matter how much it hurts at the time, I should have held him. I didn't have a chance to say goodbye the way I wanted to. I want everyone to know how important this is. Being scared is normal, but hold your child anyway!"
Michelle Butts, Mother of Austin D. Butts , born February 2, 1997
Died April 5, 1997 to SIDS

"It was the most devastating thing I have ever experienced. I have many friends who tried to help but they don't understand the impact his life and death has had on our life."
Kathy Rose, Mother of Forrest Rose , born December 30, 1996
Born still at 40 weeks gestation

"I don't know how the world continues on. How do we function when we feel such unbearable pain? Sometimes I wish I could go to sleep and not wake up for a year."
Liza Nolan, Mother of Emily Ann Nolan , born September 9, 1997
Born still at 40 weeks gestation unknown cause

"I wish I had known to open his eyes in the hospital and take pictures."
Marj Wagner, Mother of Adam Wagner
Born still 1982 at 38 weeks gestation

"Many people will look for the "old you" especially friends and family. They will expect you to turn back to where you were before. In reality, this will not happen. It can't. You have been to a different place in life now and it does change your life forever. This does not mean you won't grow-it means you will grow in another direction. This is hard for some to accept. You must be patient with yourself and realize that they do not understand and may not ever understand. If they have not been there...well, it's just hard for them to see.
Paula Mikkelson, Mother of Eric Christopher Mikkelson *, Born November 21, 1993*
Born still at 36 weeks gestation

"I felt so cheated and angry. I had so many hopes and dreams for him. There is not a day that I don't think about him and miss him. I keep a picture of him on my dresser. Even though he is not here, he continues to be my strength."
Sharon Toppin, Mother of Phillip Toppin *, born November 4, 1995*
Born still at term

"We decided to interrupt our sons pregnancy at six months. Nissuma had trisomy 13, a genetic disorder that is incompatible with life. He had neurological, cardiac and kidney problems and would have suffered tremendously. But the decision that has affected our lives the most profoundly is that I did not hold him when he died. I felt I couldn't handle the pain or the memories it would leave with me. I wish I had someone there that could tell me how much I'd regret that decision later. Nissuma deserved to be held by his mother, physically, for even just a short time. To all the parents going through this, you **can** handle holding your baby. And to Nissuma, I hold you everyday in my thoughts, my heart and my prayers."
Mike and Tami Strauss, Parents of Nissuma Strauss *, Born April 4, 1997*
Born at six months gestation, Trisomy 13

"When John died, a cross was nailed to our backs. It was heavy and we had no direction for our long journey into grief. As we walked into a life that seemed to offer no hope, we slowly picked up our cross. We began to understand that we could choose to drag our cross in anger and bitterness, or pick it up in love and memory of our beloved son, John. Our cross is much lighter now. But it remains unseen and forgotten by all except us, John's parents."
John and Lynette Sarna, Parents of John Edmund Sarna, Jr
Born September 18, 1964, died September 24, 1984, in an automobile accident

"My wife and I decided in October that we would let nature take its course and allow God to make the decision when conception would occur. We found out in December that Gina was pregnant. We realized that there is uncertainty with our third pregnancy, but we remain hopeful. When I reflect back, I feel I have lived two lives. One, when Courtney was born and the second when Nicholas was born. I am on my third life as far as I am concerned. Hopefully, this will be the greatest one of all and the last. Everything that has happened seems as if it's been much longer than it actually has been."
Todd Beisner, Father of Courtney Lynn Beisner *, Born September 13, 1995*
Died September 13, 1995, holoproencephaly
Nicholas Allan Beisner *, Born January 2, 1997*
Died January 2, 1997, Potter's Disease

"Find someone willing to listen without judging. Don't let anyone tell you that you're crazy or out of line for your personal expressions, actions or thoughts. Only you know what you are feeling and know what you are going through after the death of your child. But first and foremost continue to love and communicate with your family."
Kellie Gatewood, Mother of Zachary Isaac Gatew ood, *Born July 11, 1994*
Died December 19, 1994, died of SIDS

"...As he slept sideways in his crib, one arm and one leg sticking out the sides, mouth wide open, did he remind you that there really are angels on this earth?"
Katie Hodge, Mother of Blake Cash , *Born September 18, 1998*
Died February 18, 2000 as a driver ran a red light and collided with Katie's car

"Though her body is gone, Camille is still with us. She is our special angel. Sharon and I have already felt her presence, and her love has already worked miracles in our lives that are too personal for us to relate."
Richard K. Olsen, Father of Camille Rayana Olsen , *Born August 17, 2000*
Died August 17, 2000 S.A.D.S. Syndrome

Are we ready for another baby?

The decision to have another child is an enormous task for bereaved parents. Some feel anxious and cannot wait to hold another baby in their arms. Others fear they would feel resentment toward a new child, unconsciously desiring the child who died.

The decision to have a subsequent child is personal and private one, but one deserving great thought and consideration. There are no textbook rules to follow that determine when it is healthy to get pregnant again. For some families, several months will be adequate time. Others, however, may not feel ready for years.

Here are some things to consider when making the decision for a subsequent pregnancy after the death of a child:

✓ Is the grief of the death of your child still unbearable? Does it still consume every moment of every day? If it does, it may be too soon for another child. Grief work is exhausting work. It would be difficult to do your grief work when so much energy is required during a subsequent pregnancy. Thus, a new pregnancy may force a woman to delay healthy bereavement responses.

✓ Are you able to laugh and smile throughout your day without feeling as if you have betrayed the memory or love of your child?

✓ Are you able to attend baby showers? Can you walk through the baby aisle in department stores? How do you feel around babies? Can you hold other people's children?

✓ What is your support system like? Do you have access to subsequent pregnancy support groups? Is your family responsive and supportive?

✓ What is your reaction to other children who would be the same age and are the same gender as your child?

Tips to survive a subsequent pregnancy:

♦ Attend a subsequent pregnancy support group. No one will understand your fears, your ambivalence, and your anxiety more than other parents experiencing the same emotions.

♦ Interview and choose an especially compassionate and understanding obstetrician and pediatrician. Make sure they know about your child's death so they will understand you're the impetus for your concerns. Be sure that they are willing to address your questions, offer support, and that they will be readily available should you need their assistance. This can make all the difference in the world for surviving a subsequent pregnancy.

♦ Initiate and design a birthing plan. Write down ways for your family and the hospital staff to accommodate you and make you more comfortable. Consider bringing a framed photograph of your deceased child to the hospital with you. Some parents say it helped make them feel as if they included their child in the birth of the new baby.

♦ Apnea monitors are options to consider for extra assurance especially for high-risk or preterm infants. Most hospitals are happy to answer your questions about the monitors.

♦ Include a section in your new baby's birth book about your deceased baby. Include photographs and information so that when he or she grows up, they too will know their older sibling.

♦ Invest in a video baby monitor. Many parents report that this one product saved them a great deal of worry and stress. Some video monitors are so sensitive that you will be able to hear your baby breathing. You will also be able to see your baby. This visual aid allows many parents to feel more comfortable while their child is napping.

Surviving a subsequent pregnancy is no easy task. It can be filled with apathy, ambivalence, excitement, and bittersweet emotions. One thing is certain; it will be worth it! You will have another baby to love and cherish. And while your new child will never replace your deceased child, he or she will be a precious gift to your family.

Interplanetary Grief
Maintaining Communication and Respect

Remember the best selling book, "Men are from Mars, Women are from Venus?" The same concept can be true for grief. Many men speak a different grief language than their partners and vice versa.

There is a delicate balance to be maintained in a relationship when couples experience a significant grief event, particularly the death of their child. Life does go on, but normalcy on any level, personal and interpersonal, is challenging after the death of a child. As human beings, the basic elements of our psyche are vastly diverse. It makes sense that in stressful situations, we may not all react in the same manner. However, there are some general responses reported by many families who are bereaved. Many men see the loss as a "big picture," while many women, very specifics oriented, deduce and analyze even the tiniest of details. While this may be a broad generalization of gender responses, most often fathers report that they 'think' and most mothers report that they 'feel.' He may appear to be more logical and realistic about the events while she may describe herself as deeply intuitive and idealistic. Fathers often cope with stress and grief internally while the mother often copes externally, such as a support group setting.

Statistically, women attend for support groups for longer periods of time and are generally more communicative during the group session. While a mother and father may handle the grief intrinsically unique from the other, both need the opportunity to express their feelings. The love they share for their child should transcend any gender differences. Some fathers express a "making of peace" with the child's death between three to nine months. Most mothers, however, do not report that feeling of acceptance for two years, or longer.

Helping a Grieving Mother
A grieving mother may need to talk about the event surrounding her child's death repeatedly. She is in the process of gathering every detail about the baby's death. She is playing the tape in her mind and rewinding it over and over again. She will ask questions that may be unanswerable, such as how or why? Be patient and offer to attend a support group meeting with her. She may want to visit the grave frequently. She may even feel that this is her only way to "take care" of her child. The cemetery is a tangible place where she can care for the only physical connection to her child that remains. Encourage her to visit as often as she wants. Offer her companionship when she needs it and privacy when she asks for it.

Many mothers benefit from reading books on grief. Buy her a few books to share together. She knows in her heart that her life and the life of her family will never be the same. Acknowledge her pain, respect her feelings of deep loss and try not to rush her healing or offer a quick-fix-it. She will accept the tragedy in her own time. Don't presume that she needs professional intervention because she has a desire to talk about her child. Open dialogue keeps the child's memory alive and helps her along the grief journey.

Helping a Grieving Father
The socialization of young boys in our society often admonishes men for showing emotions. Thus, into adulthood, some men, unlike women, may feel more uncomfortable discussing

the death of their child. It may too deep and emotional. Modern anthropological research on roles identifies the father role as the culturally recognized "Protector" and "Stronghold" of the family. By society's standards, it is his duty to remain strong and unyielding: Even if his heart is breaking, he may have difficulty expressing it openly. Do not pressure him to verbalize his feelings, but simply listen when he does need to talk. If you attempt to comfort him while he is grieving, he may feel guilty for making you bear the burden of the "Protector" and quickly clean up his tears and move on to busy work. Remember that just listening is an effective way to support a grieving father.

Fathers generally indulge in hobbies, work, or other activities that take their minds off the pain. He may need space to grieve in his own way, so try to avoid imposing alternate feelings of "what should be" on him. Often, a father expresses the desire to put things back to the way they were before and for his partner to become the person she was before the child's death. This may lead to conflict because the mother's perspective may be that things will never be the same. Honest communication and mutual respect will help.

Shared but Challenging Feelings
While some parents take comfort in their faith in God, others may have overwhelming feelings of anger toward God. They may express that the death of a child invalidates their faith and religion. Feelings of anger are a normal and healthy constituent of grief. Do not discredit those feelings. Feelings are not right or wrong, they just are. Most families will work out the feelings of anger if they are doing their "grief work."

Here is an exercise that may assist partners in grief:

1. Write down the emotions and elements that are unique for the mother's grief versus the elements that are unique for the father's grief. Then write down the elements of grief you have in common.

2. Establish three-one hour periods per week. Dedicate one hour to express the common elements of grief you shared the week prior. Dedicate the next hour to share one hour of intimacy where the death of your child is not discussed. Finally an hour dedicated to sharing with family members and other children the feelings of loss you have.

With honesty, respect, communication, and love families can remain together, united and strong. Give one other permission to grieve in your own way and in your own time. Honor the differences and embrace the similarities. Family arguments in the years following the death of a child may not seem relevant to the tragedy. However, it is impossible to discount the depth of the devastation after the death of a child. There may be issues of protracted, unresolved grief or blame that manifest in unrelated arguments.
If you feel your marriage is in trouble, don't wait to seek help. Counseling with a therapist or psychologist trained in grief support and marital issues with help.

Am I Still a Big Sister and Big Brother?
The grief of children

"How many brothers do you have?" they ask her.
"I have three brothers," she says.
"Wow! And how many sisters do you have?" they ask again.
"I have one sister. But she's in Heaven," she replies proudly.

Those are words that made my eyes fill up with tears when I heard them. My daughter, then six years old, has fearless strength I often envy. Her "matter of fact," comfortable, attitude about her younger sister's death and her willing honesty made me proud that day. I knew her outlook was healthy despite the often-astonished looks she would draw from unsuspecting inquisitors. How do you help children through the grief process toward a healthy reconciliation after the death of a sibling?

In retrospect, I tried to assist my sons and daughter to deal with the sudden death of their infant sister. The most difficult aspect was discussing her death and explaining what "death" is. I was very cautious about specific terminology. Honesty is the best response. I never associated death with sleeping. I told them that their sister died, explaining that when you die, you do not ever come back on this earth. I told them that they would not see her again (if you espouse to a spiritual belief system, this may be a good opportunity to open the dialogue about those values). Use discretion when discussing God and death. Avoid the common mistake of telling the children that 'God took the child.' It may create feelings of fear, anxiety, or anger toward God. Encourage questions, ask them open-ended questions, and support an open-door policy for communication. Children may be too frightened to ask difficult questions without your reassurance. Keep your answers honest, straightforward, and simple.

Our family did share an 'open emotion' policy. I allowed myself to cry, wherever and whenever I felt the need to. I set an example for them: The expression of emotions is healthy grieving. My willingness to be open about the deep feelings of grief validated their own feelings of loss and despair. It confirmed that they could come to me when they felt overwhelmed and needed to cry, too. Sometimes, when I felt they were having a particularly challenging day, I encouraged them to cry, yell, write, draw, punch a pillow, or accompany me on a walk. On several occasions when they wanted to draw a picture or write a letter, we delivered it that day to their sister's grave. This ritual seemed to be very healing for them.

Another helpful idea for siblings is to offer them a 'special' remembrance token of their sibling for them to keep. It is a tangible reminder of a relationship that will never be forgotten. Every Christmas, our children choose a special ornament in memory of their sister to hang on our tree. It is engraved with her name and the year. They know that even though she is not here with us, that she is still a part of our family.

I always recommend that children who experience grief see a child psychologist, at least once, for assessment. Often, parents are so consumed with their own feelings of grief and loss that children are overlooked or their cries for help are misinterpreted. In addition, organizations, such as the MISS Foundation, may offer children's grief support groups and special camps. These are very helpful in affirming that they are not alone in their sadness.

Reassure your children they are still a "big brother" or "big sister." Reassure them they always will be. Make time to reminisce together. Cheyenne's pictures still hang on our walls. They are a permanent fixture in our home. She is a significant part of our family and I don't want them to ever forget her or her place in our family. Children have a simple gift of discernment in grief. Everyday, I strive to become more and more like my children.

Note: If your child experiences:
1. Extended periods of depression in which he or she loses interest in daily activities and events
2. Inability to sleep, loss of appetite, prolonged fear of being alone
3. Acting much younger for extended periods of time
4. Withdraws from friends at school
5. Sharp drop in performance or refusal to attend school

These are potential warning signs which indicate professional intervention may be needed. Please seek a therapist who specialized in grief and trauma.

When I was three years old by Stevie Jo Cacciatore
8 years old, October 1999

When I was three years old my mom had a baby
Her name is Cheyenne.

She is my only sister, but she died.
My mom cried a lot of tears.
It took a long time, but we feel better now.

My mom's heart, and my heart is still broken though.
My sister would be in kindergarten this year
She would be five years old. I wish she were alive right now.
I would love her, and play with her, and take care of her.
All we can do now is miss her.

Even though she is not with us, I love her and my mom loves her too.
We keep her close in our heart.

Love,
Stevie Jo, Cheyenne's big sister

Acts of Courage and Strength: Rethinking Modern Definitions

What characteristics define courage and strength? Many would respond by saying that courage is facing inherent fears and that strength relates to a person's ability to perform difficult tasks.

For example, a person with an intense fear of heights would be courageous to parachute from an airplane, wouldn't she? Instead of running from the debilitating fear, she stood and faced it. A person with demonstrative strength, perhaps a professional body builder, will not run from a challenge. He works out everyday, learning the skills necessary to increase his potential and toning muscles in preparation to lift that arduous bar bell.

The death of a loved one is every human being's nemesis. Thus, the resultant grief process, requiring tremendous courage to face and monumental strength to endure, has captivating similarities to the physical challenges posed to athletes. Yet, while athletes are admired and revered by society, many families in the grief process say they feel isolated within their own community. There is a misconception that deep emotions of sorrow and grief should be repressed- that a person who openly shares tears is powerless and vulnerable.

True, there are some individuals brandishing the apparent 'carry-on-chin-up' stoic posture after a death in their family. Some are commended on how well they are doing with pat-on-the-back encouragement. They are praised for their courage and strength. They have seemingly carried on with life and put the tragedy behind them. They may be admired for maintaining their composure, mistaking this business-like acumen for courage and strength. Others, the closet-grievers, are surreptitious with their emotions because they think others will view them as weak.

But a closer look at the real defining characteristics of courage and strength tells a different story. Does it take more courage and strength to bury the frightening and overwhelming emotions? Or does it take more courage and strength to deal with the grief- to look into the face of sorrow- to stare into the heart of pain? Only those who have wept **really wept** from the depths of the soul can answer that. Is there any emotion more harrowing, intimidating, and physically exhausting than those experienced during times of grief? Certainly not.

Perhaps, the definition of courage and strength should be expanded to include the person who faces their grief and who doesn't deny feelings of sorrow. The one who stands and faces the inconceivable challenges of grief and isn't afraid to share the raw emotions with others; this type of courage and strength encourages understanding and compassion- this type of courage and strength come from a person who will reach out to others in grief and help to carry another. Perhaps, those are the true defining attributes of absolute courage and strength.

When the Storm Hits: An Analogous Look at Trauma

Black skies, violent winds of change, and ominous clouds darken the heavens. A virulent hurricane will tear apart a city, savagely destroying buildings and homes, changing the 'personality' and constitution of that town. It transforms serenity to chaos, security to instability, normalcy to turmoil. The storm of grief will do the same. It wreaks havoc within the soul of a person, ruthlessly tearing apart our ideals, our innocence, and our sense of immunity. It awakens questions of faith and spirituality. Grief has the ability to alter the very essence of our character.

Sudden death strikes a family like unrelenting lightning during a torrential monsoon. It is a tragedy no one expects to face during a lifetime- an unspoken disquietude- a subliminal nightmare. Families are never prepared to deal with the death of their child. How can a person possibly prepare for a storm of this enormity? Once the deluge has passed, there is a deafening silence in the city. Disbelief of the immensity of the loss begins to settle in. Like zombies, people search for their homes, their belongings, perhaps for a loved one: remnants of their former life. Residents roam the streets, sharing the pain of their neighbors. Far away communities send assistance to survivors of the hurricane. They send food, water, and medical care: All the practical support they can offer. But not experiencing the storm themselves, they can never fully comprehend the psychological repercussions of the storm's aftermath. The survivors will find the most comfort and solace in sharing the terror of the storm with their neighbors, for they too experienced the unthinkable.

The news will feature footage of the town's renovation. Outsiders will observe the camera's perspective of the apparent revival. Seemingly, if the town looks 'normal' once again, it is presumed that life for the people is once again good. However, while the "town" will slowly rebuild, the resonant memories of the tragedy remain blazed in the hearts of the survivors. No one can forget how the storm mercilessly inscribed its presence. Buildings re-emerge, but can never feel or appear exactly as they did before the storm. New homes will be constructed, but in absence of the irreplaceable memories the former houses secretly held precious within its walls.

It is likely that grief has left parent's feeling as if their 'town' has been destroyed, their constitution dismantled. They feel 'rebuilt' (reborn) as a new 'home' (person). It will take time, hard work, and a lot of patience to reacquaint themselves with the new 'home" they live in. To get to know whom they have become after the storm of grief. Eventually, the renovation is complete. New moments of joy are reborn within the lives, homes, and buildings of the new community. The residents will never forget the thunderous demon that changed lives so dramatically. But eventually tranquility and security are rediscovered within the covenant beauty of the storm's gift- the rainbow: A promise of renewed faith, joy, and a discovery of self.

"In order to experience the rainbow, we must first survive the storm."

Candlelighting Ceremony: A Poem for Ritual

Today we light this candle
    As we remember you

For time cannot take efface
    Our love remaining true,

Today we light this candle
    So the heavens up above

Know this flame will burn forever
    Death defeated by our love,

And though we're not together
    Though our worlds are oceans apart

You will always be our angel
    Keep you close within our heart,

Today we light this candle
    To remember through each night

You're our morning sun and evening star
    The one celestial light,

As so our love until the time
    When together we shall soar,

This little candle which we light
    Means we'll love you forevermore...

Tree Planting Ceremony: A Nature Eulogy

Our Dearest Child _____,

Today, we come together to dedicate this tree you. Every moment of every day, we remember you. Though our lives continue on, the emptiness within our spirit remains untouched.

The **roots** of this tree signify our commitment to your memory, sweet child...unwavering and inherent. The **body** of this tree represents who we have become since your death. Though time and weather may alter the physical appearance of the tree, the roots remain constant and unchanging. As the body of the tree becomes stronger, the roots become stronger. Just like this tree, when we become stronger and more anchored in our journey we are less likely to succumb to the changes of the wind. The love and dedication for our child grows and strengthens. We become more secure and confident in our grief and less fearful to share with others this love we carry our lifetime. The **leaves** represent a new and changing life. The day our child died, many of us feel we died with them. We become unfamiliar with our former world. New leaves will eventually grow. We are transformed into a different person. Although this transformation is long and painful, we travel the road of new leaves together, in unity.

When you are filled with sorrow and pain; remembrance and reflection; confusion and longing, come to this tree. Spend quiet time in this place remembering your precious child. Even though the roots of this tree remain invisible to the eye, the roots there are firmly planted. So, too, your child remains with you, unseen, but ever present. Your love is truly stronger than death.

In the Spirit

In the spirit of remembrance we hold and cherish you within
In the spirit of faith, that we will see you once again,

In the spirit of friendship, when the others walk away
In the spirit of strength, helping others find their way,

In the spirit of courage, as painfully we share
In the spirit of kindness, reaching out to show you care,

In the spirit of our children shining down from up above
As we dedicate this special tree in the Spirit of Our Love.

Busiculous

Joanne Cacciatore, National MISS Foundation © 2001

"Whosoever survives the test, whatever it may be, must tell his story. That is his duty"

Busiculous. Strange word, isn't it? Someone asked me how I was when I returned from a conference I taught in Oceanside, California. After only three days, I returned home to the MISS office with 385 emails (after sorting through the advertisements) and all three voice mails were full. I was four lessons behind in my university work, had a grant proposal to turn in for the 2001 retreat, and my own four children who missed me and wanted attention. My response to her question, "How are you?" was not the rhetoric she expected. Instead, I invented a new word. Busiculous. Ridiculously busy.

I have always been a busy person. I function best that way. I am action and results oriented. None of this all-talk-no-follow-through for me. When I commit to a cause, my personal integrity holds me to my word at any sacrifice.

My closest B.C. friends (Before Cheyenne) (all bereaved parents know their lives are split into two parts: the before and after) seem to have difficulty grasping and accepting the work I do. "Why do you keep doing this?" "Can't you just go back to work at a real job?" "How long are you going to keep this up?" "All this death can't be good for you?" They flood me with inquisitions about my future plans outside of the MISS Foundation. They presumptuously conclude my mental health is at risk.

"Why **do** I do this?" I ask myself. This year, the 50 volunteers hours a week have exploded into 100. As MISS becomes more entrusted to the community, more people are calling on us to help. I can tell anecdotal tragedies: A precious baby whose life was taken by cancer, a sweet boy who was accidentally run over by his grandfather, a handsome boy who drowned in his neighbor's pool, a beautiful baby girl who died just before birth. There are countless horrors of the little prince who died in a fatal car accident, an innocent toddler who strangled in a drawstring cord, an adorable little girl who become rapidly ill and died of pneumonia, the tiny baby boy who was born to early to breathe on his own, and perfect little girl who died while trying to get out of her crib. The stories go on and on. Why **do** I do this?

I remember the days after Cheyenne died. I never slept. My body ached for my missing piece. I would pace the hallways like an animal, my arms aching, burning for my little girl. They felt like concrete and dragged in agony. I would sit in the dark on the closet floor, rocking back and forth, my knees drawn to my chest. One month after her death, I was a meager 92 lbs. I did not want to live any longer. Her nursery sat, collecting dust. The silence of that room screamed at me, taunting me.

Then one day, when I knew if I didn't get help, surely I would die from the pain, I grabbed the yellow pages and turned the light on in the closet at 2:00 a.m. I began looking for help. I knew this was more than I could handle alone. I called six phone numbers of nonprofit groups, all of which were disconnected. Except one. The Compassionate Friends. I got a recording. In desperation, barely getting the words out, I left my number. Early the next day, a volunteer from TCF called me. I was no longer alone on the journey.